Juvenile Crime

Look for these and other books in the Lucent Overview Series:

Child Abuse

Children's Rights

Death Penalty

Drug Abuse

Drugs and Sports

Drug Trafficking

Family Violence

Gangs

Homeless Children

Juvenile Crime

Police Brutality

Prisons

Juvenile Crime

by Roger Barr

LUCENT
BOOKS

LUCENT Overview Series

Library of Congress Cataloging-in-Publication Data

Barr, Roger, 1951–
    Juvenile crime / by Roger Barr.
        p.   cm. — (Lucent overview series)
    Includes bibliographical references and index.
    Summary: Defines juvenile crime and its causes and discusses
both punishment and prevention.
    ISBN 1-56006-198-7 (alk. paper)
    1. Juvenile delinquency—United States—Juvenile literature.
2. Juvenile justice, Administration of—United States—Juvenile
literature.   3. Juvenile corrections—United States—Juvenile literature.
[1. Juvenile delinquency.   2. Justice, Administration of.]   I. Title.
II. Series.
    HV9104.B3435   1998
    364.36'0973—dc21   97-27336
                                                                   CIP
                                                                    AC

Contents

Introduction

BECAUSE JUVENILES ARE not treated the same as adults by American society, the justice system treats them differently as well. When dealing with juveniles, the American justice system functions much like a parent, a concept known as *parens patriae*. Just as parents are supposed to act in the best interests of their children, the justice system is supposed to consider the best interests of young people who commit crimes.

The concept of the court acting as a parent is the cornerstone of American juvenile justice. *Parens patriae* allows the juvenile court tremendous flexibility, or discretionary power, in its dealings with juveniles. In most juvenile cases, punishment is based on the court's idea of what will help the juvenile most rather than on the severity of the crime. The court can even decide that a juvenile who has committed a criminal offense should not be confined to a juvenile facility if such an action is deemed in the best interest of the juvenile.

The origins of *parens patriae*

Today's concept of *parens patriae* has evolved over centuries and faced numerous challenges. Its original meaning, "parent of the country," dates back to sixteenth-century England. At that time, if both parents in a wealthy family died, the parents' estate was managed by a special court (known as chancery court) until their children reached the age of twenty-one.

In the early 1800s, American courts borrowed and expanded this concept to deal with a wave of thefts, or property crimes, in the cities and towns. "Urban property crime by lower-class persons . . . became a major type of crime in the whole society," writes Thomas J. Bernard in his book *The Cycle of Juvenile Justice.* Young people committed much of this crime. Concern about young offenders expanded to concern about potential offenders. Bernard writes:

> Urban property crime by poor young people is the basic problem that was defined as juvenile delinquency [in the early 1800s], but a major emphasis of the emerging juvenile justice policies was on children and youths who might commit these crimes *in the future.* Poor, vagrant youths who were congregating in groups in the cities had few options besides stealing for survival. [Officials] were not especially concerned with whether these youths had actually committed these offenses yet. The emphasis became on getting them off the streets on the assumption that they would commit these offenses soon enough if they had not yet actually done so.

An early American illustration entitled "A Tenement-House Alley Gang. Candidates for Crime" suggests that poverty breeds juvenile crime.

To provide a legal basis to get potential offenders off the streets, officials expanded the English concept of *parens patriae* to apply to delinquent juveniles whose parents were still alive. On January 1, 1825, the Society for the Reformation of Juvenile Delinquents opened the New York House of Refuge in New York City. The house's purpose was to act as a concerned parent in the best interests of juveniles who were in danger of growing up in poverty or of becoming criminals.

Other cities quickly adopted this method of dealing with juveniles. Houses of refuge were opened in Boston in 1826 and in Philadelphia in 1827. By 1868, twenty houses had opened around the country, processing an estimated forty thousand to fifty thousand juveniles.

The houses of refuge particularly targeted poor juveniles. Even when juveniles committed no crime, they could be taken into custody over their parents' objections. This practice led to an Illinois court case in 1870. A boy named Daniel O'Connell had been committed to a Chicago House of Refuge because he was deemed at risk of growing up a pauper. The boy's parents objected and sued for his release. The case was decided by the Illinois Supreme Court, the highest court in the state. The court sided with Daniel's parents by deciding that he had not committed any crime. Therefore, the court could not intervene in Daniel's life and he was ordered released. The house of refuge system was soon dismantled.

The Illinois Supreme Court's decision ultimately took away the court's ability to apply the concept of *parens patriae* to juveniles. But officials did not want to abandon a concept that allowed them the power to intervene in the lives of criminal juveniles. In 1899, the Illinois state legislature created a special juvenile court, the first court of its kind in the nation. The new juvenile court restored the justice system's power of *parens patriae*.

A separate juvenile justice system

The juvenile court concept was quickly adopted by other states. By 1925, all but two states had established juvenile

Young boys steal from a merchant's cart in a turn-of-the-century photo. Before the formation of a juvenile justice system, children deemed in danger of growing up in poverty or as criminals were placed in houses of refuge.

courts, effectively creating a separate justice system for juveniles. Today, all fifty states have juvenile courts.

As the juvenile court concept approaches its one hundredth birthday, a recent increase in violent crimes committed by juveniles has refocused attention on the validity of *parens patriae*. Since 1985, the number of assaults, robberies, rapes, and homicides committed by juveniles has increased dramatically. In 1993 alone, 3,474 juveniles between the ages of ten and seventeen were arrested for homicide.

Today's concerns about *parens patriae* are different from the concerns that led Daniel O'Connell's parents to challenge the concept in the 1870s. The O'Connells challenged the court because they believed their son was serving a sentence even though he had committed no crime. Today, concerned Americans are challenging the juvenile justice system because they believe it is too lenient. Many people contend that juveniles who commit violent crimes should be treated more like adults and receive harsh punishments. As incidents of unspeakable violence increase, more and more people are questioning whether the government should abandon the concept of *parens patriae* and treat juveniles like adults in a court of law.

1

Juvenile Crime Trends

EVERY DAY IT seems the media carry shocking stories about juveniles who commit crimes. Consider these recent cases:

- In 1993 six Houston boys, ages fourteen to eighteen, were charged with raping and killing two girls, ages fourteen and sixteen, and leaving their nude bodies in a wooded area. To make sure the girls were dead, the killers strangled them and stood on their necks, a Houston police spokesperson said.

- In Chicago in 1994 two boys dropped a five-year-old boy from a fourteenth-floor window because the boy refused to steal candy for them.

- In 1995 a fourteen-year-old San Diego boy killed a twenty-year-old pizza delivery driver while attempting to rob him.

- In June 1997 a sixteen-year-old Minnesota boy shot and killed an eighteen-year-old rather than pay him two hundred dollars for a marijuana debt.

Extensive media coverage of crimes such as these has increased the nation's concern about the types of crimes committed by juveniles. As Margaret O. Hyde writes in *Kids In and Out of Trouble*,

> Not long ago, kids were considered hopelessly delinquent when they skipped a day of school, stole an apple from the

grocer, broke a window, or went joyriding one evening in the family car without permission. Today, many juveniles sell drugs, rape, rob and shoot to kill.

While juveniles do rape, rob, and kill, it is important to remember that only a small number of America's young people commit any type of crime. In 1990, the most recent year for which figures are available, 29,929,000 young people between the ages of ten and seventeen lived in the United States. During that same year 1,299,000 cases went through the nation's juvenile courts. Those cases represented just 4.3 percent of the total juvenile population in 1990. In other words, fewer than five out of every one hundred juveniles went to juvenile court during 1990 for any offense.

Property crimes

While juveniles commit many kinds of crime they most often commit property crimes. Property crimes involve the theft or damage of property. According to the Federal Bureau of Investigation (FBI), 549,230 juveniles were arrested for property offenses in 1995. Property crimes represented nearly 27 percent of all juvenile arrests that year, more than any other type of juvenile crime.

The property crime most frequently committed by juveniles in 1995, according to the same organization, was larceny, or simple theft. In 1995, juvenile arrests for larceny numbered 379,814. Burglary, which involves entering a building to commit theft, was the second most common property crime committed by juveniles in 1995. Statistics indicate that 100,192 juveniles were arrested for burglary that year. Juveniles arrested for vandalism numbered 99,639 and motor vehicle theft arrests totaled 62,342.

Ironically, just as the media seem to be publishing more stories about juvenile crime, statistics suggest that the rate of property crimes committed by juveniles has been slowing. According to the Office of Juvenile Justice and Delinquency Prevention (OJJDP), a government organization that tracks juvenile crime rates, property crimes involving juveniles increased by 22 percent between 1985 and 1994. But the rate of increase between 1990 and 1994 was only 7 percent, and no increase was recorded between 1993 and 1994.

Property crime rates show similar trends in specific categories. Larceny cases increased 17 percent between 1985 and 1994 but only 1 percent between 1993 and 1994. Burglary rates have declined in recent years. The number of burglaries processed in juvenile court in 1994 was 5 percent lower than in 1993. Motor vehicle thefts, which show a 69 percent increase between 1985 and 1994, increased only 3 percent between 1993 and 1994.

No one knows why the number of property crimes committed by juveniles has decreased. However, the decline corresponds with a general decrease in property crimes committed by adults during the same years. Some researchers suggest that a strong economy might explain lower property crime rates. When times are good, researchers suggest, property crimes decrease because people have more money to buy goods and are less likely to steal.

Violent crime on the rise

While property crimes committed by juveniles seem to be decreasing, statistics show that violent crime is increasing. Perhaps most disturbing is the dramatic rise in the number of juveniles arrested for homicide. In 1970, 1,353 juveniles were arrested for homicide, according to FBI statistics. Juvenile arrests for homicide in 1995 numbered 2,505. Compared with 1970, arrests in 1995 increased by 85 percent.

Violent juvenile crime includes more than homicide. Government statistics show that juvenile arrests for robbery, rape, and aggravated assault have also increased in recent years. In 1970, 3,223 arrests for forcible rape were reported, compared with 4,118 in 1995, an increase of 28 percent. Statistics show that robbery arrests among juveniles also increased between 1970 and 1995, with 29,363 arrests in 1970 and 44,184 in 1995, a 50 percent increase. In the same period, arrests for aggravated assault (an attack on another person with a weapon) increased by 203 percent, jumping from 20,919 in 1970 to 63,374 in 1995.

Experts have linked these increases to several trends. One of the most significant is the growth of street gangs.

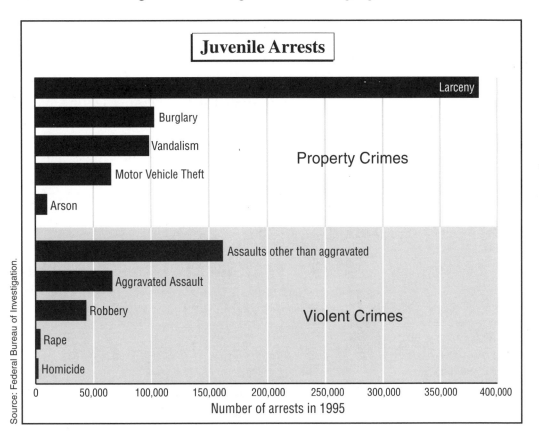

Their numbers have increased as has access to guns, another factor blamed for greater youth involvement in violent crime. A third trend involves young women. Female juveniles commit more violent crime today than previous generations of young women.

Gangs

A significant amount of the juvenile violence in America today is connected in some way to gangs. According to government statistics, 18.1 percent of all homicides in 1979 were gang related, while gangs were involved in 43 percent of homicides in 1994. Although not *all* gang-related homicides are committed by juveniles, studies in cities around the nation suggest that juveniles commit a significant portion of gang-related homicides.

The connection between homicide, juveniles, and gang activity was documented in a study in Minneapolis, Minnesota. That study covered a period from January 1, 1994, to May 24, 1997, and included the city's highest-ever homicide rate. In 1995, a record 97 homicides were committed in Minneapolis, followed by 85 homicides in 1996. During those two and a half years, almost 45 percent of the city's 264 homicides were identified as gang related. Among the 136 individuals arrested or viewed as suspects in gang-related homicides, 30 were between the ages of fourteen and seventeen, representing 22 percent of the total number of individuals linked to gang-related homicides.

A gang member hangs out with his cohorts in Derry, New Hampshire. Gangs commit a significant number of homicides in the United States each year.

Of 38 juveniles arrested for homicide or viewed as suspects, 30 were linked to gangs by investigators. Although only 4 percent of the city's juveniles belong to gangs, juvenile gang members were believed responsible for 12 percent of all homicides in the two and one-half years covered by the study. In addition, juveniles with gang ties were linked to 78.9 percent of the homicides in which a juvenile was arrested or viewed as a suspect. Although gangs have existed in the United States for generations, such incidents of violence are a fairly recent part of gang life. Those who study street gangs look for trends that might explain the increase in violent crime.

The focus of their lives

Studies indicate that the nature of gang membership has changed over the years. In bygone years, many juveniles formed a "gang" that was little more than a label for a group of friends. Today juveniles form or join gangs for various reasons. Some juveniles join gangs simply because they are looking for excitement. Juveniles who live in neighborhoods with high crime rates or neighborhoods populated with other gangs often join a gang for protection.

Studies also indicate that once today's juveniles join a gang, the gang often becomes the focus of their lives. The gang became the focus of seventeen-year-old José Chairez's life. Chairez told his story from the DeWitt Nelson Training Center in Stockton, California, where he was serving a five-year sentence for stabbing a twenty-year-old man to death in December 1992. After starting Yerba Buena High School in San Jose, California, Chairez joined a gang called VSJ, which stood for Varrio San Jose. For a time, he continued to attend classes. He even played high school football and held a part-time job. But the bond with fellow gang members eventually won out over school, football, and work. "Basically, I took that choice of hanging around with the guys," he said, "and that's how I got caught up in all the gang activity. And it's what led to my crime—being in the gang."

When gang members commit violent crimes, these crimes can often be tied to issues of respect. For many gang members the gang provides a sense of respect that they cannot find elsewhere. In *Do or Die* author Léon Bing documents the importance of respect in gang activities. Members of one Los Angeles gang cite lack of respect as a reason for killing. Gang members said they would kill another person if he "give me no respect" or if "he called me a baboon—dis' me" or if "I don't like his attitude."

Gang violence is also associated with territory. Gangs stake out portions of their neighborhoods and defend them against other gangs, using acts of violence if necessary. In *Do or Die* gang members said that acts that inspired retaliation included "wearin the wrong color [signifying membership in another gang]" or being "a transformer [a spy] in my hood."

Many gangs are involved in the drug trade, but gang violence is not believed to be strongly related to drugs. Several studies have shown only casual connections between street gangs, drugs, and homicide rates. For example, a 1993 study of two small cities near Los Angeles, California, indicated that gang members were involved in about 27 percent of arrests for cocaine sales and about 12 percent of arrests connected to other drug sales. Only 10 percent of the cases involved firearms and only 5 percent of the cases involved violence. A 1993 study of Chicago's four largest and most criminally active street gangs found only 8 of 285 gang-related homicides between 1987 and 1990 were related to drugs.

Carrying guns

Another trend that has contributed to the increase in violence among juveniles is the availability of dangerous weapons—particularly guns. Because firearms carried by juveniles are often obtained illegally, it is difficult to estimate how many firearms are in the possession of juveniles nationwide. However, arrest rates for juveniles possessing firearms have risen sharply across the nation. In New York City in 1985, for example, fewer than two hundred young people under the age of sixteen were arrested for possessing a loaded gun. Six years later, arrests for the same offense had nearly quadrupled.

Nationally, statistics indicate that juveniles are not only carrying firearms, but using them with deadly results. Figures from the FBI show that the number of homicides committed by a juvenile with a firearm increased dramatically

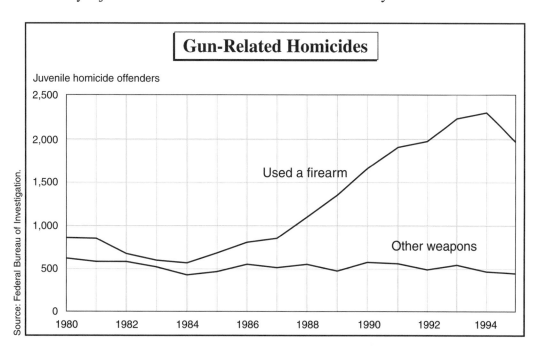

Source: Federal Bureau of Investigation.

between 1984 and 1995. Juveniles committed about six hundred gun-related homicides in 1984 compared with 1,952 similar homicides in 1995. The latter number accounts for over three-fourths of all homicides committed by juveniles that year.

Anecdotal evidence suggests that many young people, especially in urban areas with high crime rates, carry firearms for protection. Such was the case with "Andre," a New York City teenager whose story appears in the book *Kids and Guns: A National Disgrace*. At the time of the book's publication in 1993, Andre was serving a life sentence for homicide. After repeated beatings by a group of boys in his neighborhood, Andre obtained a gun. He describes his next encounter with them:

> I had the gun behind my back but [one of them] could see it. I'm telling him to back away or else I'm going to have to shoot. I was petrified I was going to get jumped. The guy said, "If you shoot me, you better kill me because I'll get you." I didn't intend to kill him, I just wanted to scare him. I didn't know it would go off so easily.

A status symbol

Some juveniles carry firearms to enhance their status among their peers and to obtain a sense of power. In August 1993 *Time* magazine explored a growing trend of juvenile gun ownership in the suburbs of Omaha, Nebraska. The article, entitled "A Boy and His Gun," told the story of Doug (not his real name), who purchased a used Remington semiautomatic 12-gauge shotgun for twenty-five dollars. The gun made Doug feel powerful. "If you have a gun, you have power," Doug told *Time*. "That's just the way it is. You fire a gun and you can just hear the power."

In the space of four months, Doug estimated, he committed nine drive-by shootings, aiming mostly at cars and houses. "I'm not actually aiming at anybody," Doug said. He views guns, he said, as "just a part of growing up these days" in the Omaha area.

The story of Doug and his gun caused a national sensation. Following the article's publication, Omaha's deputy police chief said that *Time*'s reporters had sensationalized

"When your Grandma Constance and I were your age, we didn't have automatic weapons."

and over-dramatized the problem of guns and youth in the Omaha area. But a survey in another part of the country conducted by researchers Joseph F. Sheley and Victoria E. Brewer suggested that guns are becoming a significant part of youth culture in suburban communities. Sheley and Brewer published their study in 1995. They found that nearly one in five Jefferson Parish, Louisiana, students owns a handgun. Unlike urban youths, who cite protection as a primary reason for carrying guns, Jefferson Parish students carry guns to enhance their status among their peers, the researchers concluded.

> Those who own handguns do not inhabit discernibly more hostile environments than do nonowners—beyond the danger that characterizes the violent criminality of owners of automatic or semiautomatic weapons. Nor are those who carry handguns more likely the products of dangerous surroundings, independent of involvement in drug and criminal activity.

The researchers suggested that suburban students may be caught up in a fad, noting that while "urban youth and serious juvenile offenders rather clearly are not highly motivated to possess guns for status enhancement, perhaps suburban youth are."

A female gang member of the Circle City Piru Bloods poses in a threatening manner. When teenagers obtain weapons, they are more likely than adults to use them.

Whatever the reason for carrying firearms, most experts agree firearms in the hands of juveniles are more dangerous than in the hands of adults. Teenagers tend to be impulsive and rash, often acting with little or no consideration for the consequences of their actions. Writing in the January 1994 issue of *USA Today* magazine, criminal justice experts James Alan Fox and Glenn Pierce observe that

> A 14-year old armed with a gun is far more menacing than a 44-year old with the same weapon. While the teen may be untrained in using a firearm, he is more willing to pull the trigger—without fully considering the consequences. Also the gun psychologically distances the offender from his victim. It is all too easy—just pull the trigger.

The growing presence of guns among teenagers increases the likelihood of a tragic outcome in what might otherwise be a loud but harmless argument. In January 1997, for example, a seventeen-year-old St. Paul, Minnesota, youth named Kao Lor shot and killed his older brother during an argument over a video game. According to Sgt. Brock Ness, a St. Paul police officer, the gun made the difference between a fight and a homicide. "I used to fight with my sister over whose turn it was to do the dishes," Ness said. "The difference is I used to roll up a wet towel and whack her, not use a gun."

Violent female offenders

Another trend that researchers have linked to the nation's rising rate of violent juvenile crime is the increase in crimes committed by girls. While boys commit most violent offenses, researchers have observed an increase in violent crimes committed by girls. In the past, girls were primarily observers of violence committed by boys. Now they appear to be perpetrators of violence rather than mere observers. Many juvenile crime statistics do not distinguish gender, making it hard to determine how crime patterns of female offenders have changed in recent years.

Available data indicates that the number of violent offenses committed by juvenile females is increasing. The nation's law enforcement agencies made an estimated 482,039 arrests involving juvenile females in 1995. That year, juvenile females made up 6 percent of juvenile arrests for homicide, 2 percent of arrests for forcible rape, 9 percent of robbery arrests, and 20 percent of aggravated assault arrests. Arrests of juvenile females for violent crimes in 1995 rose by 124 percent over 1986.

Statistics indicate that although the violent crime rate for juvenile females still lags far behind that of juvenile males, it is growing at a faster rate. For example, between 1986 and 1995, the arrest rate for females grew by 124 percent, compared with a growth of 60 percent for males. During those years, the female proportion of all juvenile arrests grew from 22 percent to 26 percent—about one arrest in every four.

Researchers have evaluated statistics and case studies of individual female offenders in their search for clues that might explain this change. They have found at least one common experience among young female offenders: a troubled childhood. Researcher Ilene R. Bergsmann draws this composite of a typical female offender:

Young women in trouble with the law are typically 16 years old, live in urban ghettos, are high school dropouts, and are victims of sexual and/or physical abuse or exploitation. Most come from single parent families, have experienced foster care placement, lack adequate work and social skills, and are substance abusers. Over half of these adolescent females are black or Hispanic.

A troubled childhood does not automatically guarantee that a female will become a violent offender. Researchers believe, however, that females who experience one or more of the problems identified by Bergsmann during childhood are more likely to accept violence as a part of life. Violent offenses by females are frequently associated with gang activity. It is difficult to determine how many females are gang members nationwide. In Los Angeles alone, according to one estimate, females comprise approximately 15 percent or about six thousand of the city's gang population.

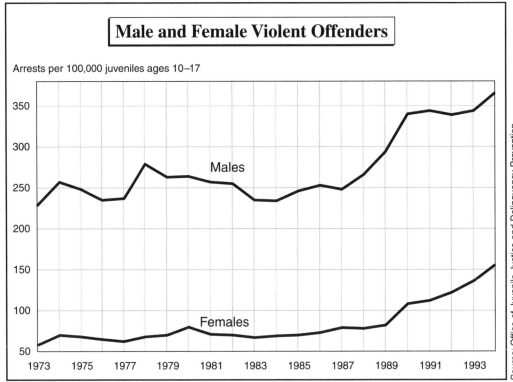

Male and Female Violent Offenders

Arrests per 100,000 juveniles ages 10–17

Males

Females

Source: Office of Juvenile Justice and Delinquency Prevention.

As with juvenile males, membership in a gang can lead a juvenile female to violent behavior. The story of Jackee, which appeared in the August 1995 issue of *Teen*, is typical of many female gang members. Jackee joined a gang in her Chicago neighborhood when she was in the eighth grade. At first, her activities consisted mostly of socializing with other gang members. "For girls, back then, it wasn't really anything," she told *Teen*. "We were just hanging out, just talking about people. We'd fight, but it wouldn't be over anything serious. We weren't seriously hurting people."

Within a few years, Jackee and her friends were committing more serious offenses. They broke car windows, vandalized property with graffiti, and sold drugs. She beat up girls in retaliation for attacks on her friends. One day while hanging out with her cousin, Sheila, a girl neither of them knew challenged Sheila to a fight. Jackee pulled out her .22-caliber pistol to defend her cousin. "I put it to the girl's head because she wanted to fight my cousin," she said.

Members of an all-girl gang meet in East Los Angeles. Girls who are involved in gangs are more likely to commit crimes.

After the gun incident, however, Jackee reevaluated her life. She got rid of the gun. She made an attempt to move away from gang life but found it difficult because it was the only world she knew.

Research suggests that girls often join male gangs through their relationships with family members, friends, or boyfriends who are already gang members. In some areas where gang activity is high, girls join to avoid harassment from other gang members. Abuse is also a factor in female gang membership. "At least 90 percent of the girls who join gangs have experienced severe emotional, sexual or physical abuse, usually by a caretaker," observes Diane Griggs, a licensed clinical social worker at the Didi Hirsch Community Mental Health Clinic in Inglewood, California. Interviewed in the July 1994 issue of *Essence*, Griggs observed that "low self-esteem and isolation keep them from trusting anyone. So they internalize the abuse and enter the gang to act out their rage and anger."

Four young girls flash their gang sign at a mall in Los Angeles. Many girls who join gangs have been emotionally, physically, or sexually abused.

In recent years, some girls have formed their own gangs. No one knows how many all-girl gangs exist in the country but gang experts believe that the number is increasing. One 1991 study found that girl gangs existed in twenty-seven American cities. Total membership in those gangs was estimated at 7,205, or 3 percent of the total gang population in those cities.

According to gang expert Rafe Cancio, female gangs can be as violent as their male counterparts. Writing in the August 1995 issue of *Teen*, Cancio states,

> In the last five years, some all-girl gangs have started to crop up and they are beginning to be as ruthless as their male counterparts. They are doing drive-by shootings. They are doing robberies. They are selling dope. And they are doing it without the need for protection from males.

The increase in violent juvenile crime over the past decade has alarmed the nation. While citing guns and gangs as contributing factors to increases in juvenile crime, many juvenile experts believe that these trends are only symptoms of deeper causes. Because young people represent the future of the nation, experts in many fields are trying to discover the exact reasons why juvenile behavior has become more violent. If the reasons can be discovered, experts reason, new strategies can be developed to fight juvenile crime.

2

Causes of Juvenile Crime

JUVENILE CRIME EXPERTS have not reached a consensus on the reasons for the increase in violent juvenile crime. Demographers, who conduct statistical studies of human populations, have pored over various statistics for millions of juveniles across the nation in search of patterns. Members of America's justice system have looked for recurring themes in the profiles of juvenile criminals. Scientists have searched for biological factors that may help explain the increase. Sociologists, criminal experts, and specialists from other fields have also joined the search, isolating various factors they believe have contributed to the increase in violent crime among juveniles.

Demographic trends

One explanation for the increase in violent juvenile crimes is the rise in the nation's juvenile population. Demographers studying population trends over many decades have found links between increases in the juvenile population and the rise in juvenile crime rates. Studies show that young males are the most likely individuals to commit crimes. As juveniles move out of their teen years their criminal activity tends to decrease. If the number of individuals in this age group increases, simple logic suggests that the number of juvenile crimes committed will also increase.

That happened during the 1960s and 1970s when the baby boomers—children born between 1945 and 1965—

reached adolescence. Juvenile crime rates went up, in part because there were more juveniles living in the country, and then leveled off as they grew out of their crime-prone years. Criminologist James Alan Fox predicted in 1975 that crime rates would fall during the 1980s after the last of the baby boomers matured. Fox also predicted that juvenile crime rates would rise again in the early 1990s as the children of baby boomers reached their teenage years.

According to population statistics, the number of juveniles in America is again rising and will increase significantly by 2005. Criminologist John DiIulio Jr. expresses concern about how these numbers will affect crime rates.

> What is really frightening everyone from D.A.s to demographers, old cops to old convicts, is not what's happening now but what's just around the corner—namely, a sharp increase in the number of super crime-prone young males.

> Nationally, there are now about 40 million children under the age of 10, the largest number in decades. By simple math, in a decade today's 4 to 7-year-olds will become 14 to 17-year-olds. By 2005, the number of males in this age group will have risen about 25 percent overall.

The anticipated surge in the juvenile population combined with the recent trend of more violent crimes being committed by juveniles has many experts concerned about the future.

Demographics can go only so far in explaining increases in juvenile crime rates. Demographic trends do not explain, for example, why juvenile crime rates began to rise dramatically about 1986—at least five years earlier than Fox predicted.

The arrival of crack

When demographers make long-range predictions, they cannot always anticipate developments that may alter human behavior and influence population trends. One such development was the introduction of crack cocaine into the United States.

In the mid-1980s crack cocaine abruptly altered the landscape of America's drug culture. Crack's popularity spread quickly. Government statistics list juvenile arrests for possession of cocaine and the drug heroin in the same category. According to the *U.S. Statistical Abstract for 1996*, juvenile arrests for possession of cocaine or heroin increased dramatically after the introduction of crack. Juvenile arrests in this category numbered 2,614 in 1980 (before crack became popular). In 1985, after its introduction, juvenile arrests for possession of cocaine and heroin totaled 7,899. Arrests nearly doubled by 1990, numbering 15,194. In 1994, arrests totaled 21,004—an eightfold increase over 1980.

Crack was easy to use, produced a quick high, and was fairly inexpensive. Crack also proved to be highly addictive. The combination of these factors made the crack trade especially lucrative and violent. It is characterized by desperate users and greedy dealers.

Juveniles became an integral part of the distribution chain that moves crack through the nation's streets. Because juveniles generally receive lighter punishment if caught, adult dealers often employ juveniles—some as young as nine or ten—to hold the drug for them, transport it from place to place, or act as scouts during drug transactions.

A man smokes crack in an alley. Drug dealers often employ juveniles to distribute and sell crack since minors usually receive lighter punishments when caught.

Law enforcement officials believe that juveniles who are recruited into the crack trade also are more likely to be armed. The National Institute of Justice (NIJ), an agency within the U.S. Department of Justice, stated this position in June 1996. "For those transporting valuable illicit merchandise, whether money or drugs, a gun was seen as necessary for protection, especially because they could not call for police assistance if threatened."

Gang members stand at their usual corner, waiting to sell drugs to passersby. Such juveniles are likely to carry firearms.

Author Deborah Prothrow-Stith, who is assistant dean of the Harvard University School of Public Health, describes the desperation and violence that fills the lives of young crack dealers on the streets of Washington, D.C.

> The life of young street-level dealers, many of whom are crack users, is a desperate and sordid affair. On the street, each person must look out for himself, each person is a predator. "Stick up boys" steal the drug supplies of other dealers. Sometimes dealers smoke up their supply of crack and say they have been robbed. Either way, dealers are always afraid, always running from someone. In Washington, D.C., suppliers punish dealers who do not pay up by beating them with baseball bats. . . . As a defensive measure, the code of the

street says everyone associated with the drug trade must routinely "exert maximum force." That means shoot to kill no matter what the provocation.

The shoot-to-kill rule among young drug dealers has been linked to an increase in the number of homicides committed by juveniles, especially those committed by nonwhite juveniles. The National Institute for Justice states that juveniles recruited into the drug trade are "primarily nonwhite youths, many of whom saw this as their only viable economic opportunity. The rate of arrests [for drug offenses among nonwhite youths] rose from approximately 200 per 100,000 in 1985 to twice that rate 4 years later." The agency also notes that the homicide arrest rate for nonwhite youths increased by 120 percent between 1985 and 1992. By contrast, according to the NIJ, the arrest rate for drug offenses for white youths declined during the same period and the homicide rate among white youths grew at a much slower rate than among nonwhite youths, who were more deeply involved in the crack industry.

Violence in the media

Violence in the media has also been identified by some experts as a cause of violent juvenile crime. Graphic depictions of violent acts can be seen in children's cartoons, in television programs and televised movies, in motion pictures, and on news programs. Barbara Hattemer writes:

> The networks provide up to 10 violent acts per hour; cable, up to 18 violent acts per hour; and children's cartoons 32 violent acts per hour. Movies like *Teenage Mutant Ninja Turtles* raise the count to 133 violent acts per hour. The body count is rising, too: *Total Recall*, 74 dead; *Robocop 2*, 81 dead; *Rambo III*, 106 dead; and *Die Hard 2*, 264 dead.

Violence is prevalent in music, particularly in rap and heavy metal, which attract mostly young listeners. Rap and heavy metal performers use explicit lyrics to address topics ranging from murder and suicide to drugs and guns. The violent content of lyrics leads to violent images in accompanying music videos, which also have a big audience among young people. The National Coalition on Television

Violence found that 45 percent of the twelve hundred rock videos it studied contained violent content.

Some experts believe that young people are vulnerable to violent images and lyrics and may incorporate the violence they see in the media into their own behavior. Supporters of this concept say that as violence in the media increases, violent juvenile crime also increases. Whether media violence inspires juvenile violent crime remains unproven.

Copycat acts, which are crimes or acts of violence that juveniles saw in the media and later repeated, are often cited as examples of media influence on crime. In 1993, for example, a five-year-old Ohio boy set a fire that killed his two-year-old sister. The boy's mother later told authorities that the boy had recently watched the MTV cartoon *Beavis and Butthead*. In the cartoon, Beavis frequently sets fires for fun.

Another copycat act occurred in 1994 following the release of the movie *Natural Born Killers*. The movie's plot concerns two young people who go on a murderous crime spree. Not long after the film's release, two teenagers, Sarah Edmonson and Benjamin Darras, went on a crime spree of their own. In Hernando, Mississippi, they shot and killed William Savage outside of the cotton gin where he

worked. The next day they robbed a convenience store in nearby Ponchatoula, Louisiana, shooting Patsy Byers, leaving her paralyzed for the rest of her life. After their arrest, Edmonson told authorities that before the shootings, she and Darras had used the drug LSD and watched *Natural Born Killers* numerous times.

Although they do not occur very frequently, copycat crimes and acts of violence receive widespread media attention. Writing in the January/February 1994 issue of the *Humanist*, Brian Siano explained why copycat crimes received such coverage:

> Stories of media-inspired violence are striking mainly because they're so *atypical* of the norm; the vast majority of people don't take a movie or a TV show as a license to kill. Ironically, it is the *abnormality* of these stories that ensures they'll get widespread dissemination and be remembered long after the more mundane crimes are forgotten.

Does violence in the media influence juvenile behavior?

Many researchers believe that links also exist between media violence and the "more mundane crimes" mentioned by Siano—the violent crimes committed by juveniles every day. According to one estimate, nearly three thousand studies have explored the relationship between media violence and violent behavior. Most of those studies have established a link between the two. One of the most well known studies found a direct link between television violence and aggressive behavior. In that study, researcher Leonard D. Eron observed that among children "there is no denying . . . the relation between television viewing and aggressive behavior" and that "aggressive behavior results in children turning more often to watching violent television programs."

Some experts fear that repeated exposure to media violence makes people, especially juveniles, more accepting of violence. Author Deborah Prothrow-Stith observes that

> children who watch a great deal of violent TV are desensitized to the wrongness of what they are seeing. Television tells them that violence is an everyday occurrence, a justified form of self-defense. Teens who live in communities where

Many analysts believe that the continuous violence that children are exposed to while watching television may cause some to become violent criminals later in life.

violence is endemic are particularly vulnerable. TV reinforces the seeming ordinariness and rightness of the violence that confronts them daily. The violence these children see on television tells them that the violence in which they live is expected and normal—when in fact it is neither.

Not everyone agrees with the idea that media depictions of violence cause increases in juvenile crime. In a study of fifteen hundred youths in the United States, Australia, Finland, and Poland, researcher Rowell Huesmann concluded that only a casual link exists between television violence and real violence. Huesmann argued that television was responsible for as little as 5 percent of the violence in society.

Others say that the blame placed on music, movies, and television is misguided and obscures more important causes of violent crime among youth. In the May 1994 issue of *USA Today*, Tricia Rose, assistant professor of history and Africana studies at New York University, defends rap music against critics who argue that it promotes violence among black youth. Rose states that

> Rap music has become a lightning rod for those politicians and law and order officials who are hell-bent on scapegoating it as a major source of violence instead of attending to the much more difficult and complicated work of transforming the brutally unjust institutions that shape the lives of poor people.

Although she disliked the content of some rap lyrics, Rose said that rap often described the world from the point of view of poor black males: "Many a gangsta rap tale chronicles the experience of wandering around all day, try-

Violent and sexually explicit lyrics, such as those found in the songs of rap singer Eazy-E, are controversial. Critics believe such music glorifies a culture of violence.

ing to make order out of a horizon of unemployment, gang cultural occupation, the threat of violence from police and rival teens, and fragile home relationships."

Biological factors

Scientists have long suspected that violent criminals may have biological or physiological differences that contribute to their violent behavior. Juveniles who commit violent crimes often have common characteristics. For example, they are unusually fearless and often take risks. They may have a short attention span and become restless quickly. Often they have trouble empathizing with others and want immediate gratification of their needs. Some researchers believe that characteristics like these may have biological origins.

Recent studies suggest several ways in which biological factors might contribute to violent behavior. A chemical imbalance is one possible influence. Serotonin, for example, helps regulate mood and emotion. Imbalances of serotonin were linked to aggressive acts in juveniles in a 1992 study conducted by Dr. Markus J. P. Kruesi. Kruesi studied a group of adolescents who exhibited disruptive behavior and found high concentrations of serotonin in their spinal fluids. He concluded that elevated levels of serotonin were an indicator of aggressive behavior.

Some juveniles who exhibit antisocial or aggressive behavior differ physiologically from their peers. They may have lower heart rates and slower brain activity, for example, which scientists believe results in lower levels of physiological stimulation. Experts suggest that such youths may act aggressively in an attempt to reach normal levels of physiological stimulation. This theory helps explain antisocial behavior such as setting fires, cruelty to animals, or destruction of objects. Such behavior often occurs among juveniles who later commit violent crimes.

Damage to the brain of a developing fetus or infant has also been linked to future criminal behavior. Brain damage can occur in different ways. A developing fetus can suffer brain damage if the mother abuses drugs or alcohol during pregnancy. Sometimes babies suffer brain damage during a difficult delivery. Children who contract lead poisoning can also suffer brain damage. An infant can contract lead poisoning by eating lead-based paint chips scraped from a wall. Lead paint was once commonly used in painting the interior of homes.

A 1990 study conducted by Deborah Denno, a law professor at Fordham University in New York City, found a connection between lead poisoning and juvenile crime. Denno found that the presence of lead poisoning in juveniles was the strongest indicator of future discipline problems in school. She also found that discipline problems in school were the best predictor of an arrest record for juveniles between the ages of seven and twenty-two.

Scientists speculate that certain types of brain damage affect the portion of the brain that helps curb aggressive impulses and the ability of the brain to process information. The result may be difficulty with comprehending the rules of society or functioning well in school.

Police officers subdue a girl after breaking up a fight. Some scientists argue that biological differences exist between juveniles who are aggressive and those who are not.

The relationship between brain damage and juvenile crime has been linked in several studies. In 1988, a study of thirteen juvenile murderers between the ages of thirteen and seventeen found that more than half had major brain dysfunction resulting from falls, accidents, or other traumas. By contrast, in a comparison group of nonviolent juveniles, researchers found that only 6 percent showed signs of brain impairment.

Although biological factors can increase the likelihood that juveniles will become violent, scientists say that this outcome is not automatic. Most researchers agree that biological factors combine with other factors, particularly the setting in which a young person lives, to produce violent behavior.

Environmental factors in violent juvenile behavior

Many experts believe that the type of environment a juvenile lives in influences his or her behavior. Researchers have identified numerous environmental factors that may trigger at-risk juveniles to become violent offenders. One such factor is a poor family life. Maltreatment, including physical abuse, sexual abuse, or neglect, is a recurring theme in the family backgrounds of many violent juvenile offenders. A study conducted in Rochester, New York, between 1988 and 1992 demonstrated a relationship between maltreatment and violent juvenile behavior. The study showed that 69 percent of the youths who had been maltreated as young children exhibited violent behavior ranging from assault to armed robbery and aggravated assault. Thirteen percent fewer juveniles (56 percent) who had not been maltreated exhibited violent behavior.

The same study indicated a strong link between multiple forms of family violence and violent juvenile behavior. In addition to studying the relationship between maltreatment and juvenile violence, the study examined the relationship between violent juvenile behavior and two other forms of family violence—incidents of violence between

the juvenile's parents and general hostility within the family. Sixty percent of the violent youths in the study had been exposed to one of three forms of family violence: maltreatment, parental violence, or other family hostility. Seventy-three percent of juveniles exposed to two forms of violence later committed violent crimes while 78 percent of juveniles exposed to all three forms of violence later committed acts of violence. Juveniles exposed to all three forms of violence were 40 percent more likely to act violently than were juveniles who were not exposed to violence.

Changes in American family structure have also been identified as contributing to rising juvenile crime rates. Traditionally, the family unit consisted of a mother and father and their children all living under the same roof. In the last half of the twentieth century, a variety of economic trends and social movements have shattered this traditional arrangement. Between 1970 and 1995 the percentage of all children living in two-parent families dropped from 85 percent to 69 percent. The decline of two-parent families was most pronounced among African Americans. Fifty-nine percent of African American children under eighteen lived with both parents in 1970 while only 33 percent lived with both parents in 1995. By contrast, 90 percent of children under the age of eighteen in white families lived with both parents in 1970, and in 1995, 76 percent lived with both parents.

Experts suggest the increase in single-parent households has resulted in inadequate care and supervision of millions of young people. Single parents are often less able to manage a household effectively and devote time to their children. Statistics indicate that the majority of single-parent households are now headed by females. The absence of fathers in households has led to many boys growing up without a male role model. The absence of a male role model is a common theme in the lives of boys who join gangs.

Single-parent families often have lower incomes, which adds emotional stress to daily life. Between 1970 and 1993, the number of American children living in poverty rose from 14.9 percent to 22 percent. Much of that

A child takes second-hand clothes to his mother, who lives in the makeshift shack on the left. Analysts believe that children who grow up in poverty and without fathers are more at risk to commit violent crimes.

increase occurred among African American families. In 1993, according to government statistics, 45.9 percent of African American children lived below the poverty line. By contrast, only 17 percent of white children lived below the poverty line.

As a result of these changes, many juveniles grow up in an environment that is both economically and morally impoverished. These disadvantages put juveniles from single-parent families at greater risk of committing crimes. According to one study, juveniles from single-parent families are 70 percent more likely to be expelled from school. They make up 70 percent of the total number of juvenile delinquents in state reform institutions. Juveniles from single-parent families are also believed to account for 75 percent of the homicides attributed to juveniles.

The links established by researchers between juvenile crime and environmental factors such as broken families and poverty do not mean that every juvenile who lives in such an environment will grow up to be a violent offender. Most juveniles who grow up in poverty or single-parent families do not commit crimes. However, experts believe that these factors help explain why violent crime is more prevalent among African American juveniles than among whites. According to the Office of Juvenile Justice and Delinquency Prevention, in 1994, African American juveniles were involved in 32 percent, or one-third, of all delinquency cases handled by U.S. juvenile courts. In contrast, African Americans represented only 15 percent of the nation's juvenile population.

A combination of factors

Most researchers believe that a combination of factors has led to an increase in violent juvenile crime rates. Often, several contributing factors can be identified in the life of a single juvenile offender. For example, in 1993 in Savona, New York, thirteen-year-old Eric Smith killed four-year-old Derrick Robie. In confessing to the crime, Eric admitted to authorities that he wanted to hurt the younger boy. An investigation into the crime found that

Eric was a slow learner as a toddler and had trouble keeping up in school. At the age of nine he tried to choke a neighbor's cat. On another occasion he started a fire with paper on the family stove. These incidents are consistent with biological and physiological factors that experts believe are indicators of violent behavior. Eric's parents admitted that they argued frequently and that the father physically and verbally abused Eric, suggesting a poor family life as another possible factor that might have triggered Eric's criminal behavior.

Determining which factors motivate a juvenile's violent offense and providing adequate punishment and treatment are among the functions of the juvenile justice system. As the number of violent offenses rises, however, the American public is growing increasingly concerned about whether the juvenile justice system is adequately equipped to meet the demands placed upon it.

3

The Juvenile
Justice System

IN FEBRUARY 1996, two sixteen-year-old Florida youths, Max Brazley and Xavien Bendross, and twenty-year-old Barry Chandler were accused of killing a Dutch tourist. Chandler, considered an adult by the law, was charged as an adult and, if convicted, faced a lengthy sentence in an adult prison. Brazley and Bendross presented authorities with a dilemma. Legally, they were not adults, yet they had been accused of a brutal and violent crime. If charged as adults, and convicted, they would face a lengthy sentence in prison. If charged as juveniles, their cases would be processed in a separate juvenile justice system that was originally designed to handle minor juvenile offenses, a system that traditionally emphasized rehabilitation over punishment.

But some would argue that the juvenile justice system had already failed in its mission to rehabilitate the youths and that this case belonged in adult court. Both Brazley and Bendross were already under supervision of the juvenile court, although neither was in custody at the time of the shooting. Brazley's first offense was in 1992, when at the age of twelve he was charged with armed robbery. By the time he reached sixteen, he had been involved in twelve cases, including grand theft and attempted armed burglary. During 1995, Brazley had been committed to a juvenile facility on three different occasions. Shortly before the murder of the Dutch tourist, Brazley completed a three-month residential program aimed at getting young offenders back on track. The court also recommended that Brazley, who had flunked nearly all of his classes over the past four years, learn to read.

Bendross had flunked eighth grade, repeated it, and although he spent only two weeks in school, had been promoted to ninth grade. In December 1995, he was placed on probation for selling crack cocaine. In February 1996, Bendross was again in juvenile court facing charges for possessing marijuana. At that appearance, the judge put him on a waiting list for an alternative school. A trial date was set for March and Bendross was sent home.

Less than twenty-four hours after Bendross's court appearance, he, Brazley, and Chandler attempted to rob two Dutch tourists at a Miami, Florida, gas station. During the robbery attempt, Brazley could not get the tourists' rental car door open, and in a fit of anger allegedly shot and killed one of them.

Three young men, two of whom are only age sixteen, are charged with the murder of a Dutch tourist and are taken into custody by police officers. The two juveniles had been in and out of the juvenile justice system for years.

This case was one of more than three thousand homicides committed by juveniles in 1996. These cases, along with scores of other violent offenses, have created a crisis in the American justice system. They have fueled a debate about whether America's juvenile justice system is adequately equipped to deal with today's violent juvenile offenders.

A separate legal system

The juvenile justice system is a separate legal system designed to handle cases involving crimes committed by juvenile offenders. Since the nation's first juvenile court was created in Illinois in 1899, the main goal of the juvenile justice system has been to rehabilitate juvenile offenders. The juvenile justice system also exists to protect the general public by incarcerating dangerous juvenile offenders so they cannot harm others.

'This must be juvenile court.'

Reprinted by permission of the *Spectator*, London.

Because they are separate from the criminal justice system, the juvenile courts operate under different procedures. The most important feature of the juvenile court system is its view of juveniles as different from adults. "The central premise of the juvenile court is that children should be treated differently from adults," write authors Barry Krisberg and James F. Austin. "The court . . . assumes that adolescents possess somewhat less responsibility for their actions and need protection."

To "protect" juveniles, the court acts as a parent to the juvenile, a concept known as *parens patriae*. As the judicial parent to the juvenile, the court is supposed to act in the best interests of the juvenile.

Unlike criminal court, juvenile court proceedings traditionally are closed to the general public. The court maintains that keeping the system closed is in the best interests of the child. The juvenile justice system operates under the belief that young offenders can be rehabilitated. According to this view, open proceedings could permanently damage young offenders' reputations and make it difficult for them to put their mistakes behind them and assume a productive place in society. Sealed records allow a young offender who is rehabilitated to enter adulthood without a criminal record.

How the juvenile justice system works

The juvenile justice system has jurisdiction in two kinds of offenses: status offenses and criminal offenses. Status offenses are based on a set of laws that apply only to juveniles. They include truancy (skipping school), running away from home, refusing to obey one's parents, violating curfew, drinking alcohol, and engaging in consensual sex. Juveniles who commit status offenses can be taken into custody and processed through the juvenile justice system.

Status offenses exist to correct undesirable behavior. The ability to enforce status offenses gives the juvenile court nearly unlimited power to intervene in the lives of young people who are at risk of committing criminal acts.

A probation officer and police officer take a juvenile into custody for violating his parole. Juvenile justice is based on the premise of rehabilitation.

When authorities arrest juveniles for status offenses they do so in the belief that such action will help deter future involvement in crime.

The juvenile court also has jurisdiction over criminal offenses committed by juveniles. Criminal offenses include murder, rape, armed robbery, aggravated assault, burglary, larceny, auto theft, and arson.

The juvenile justice system's protective attitude toward juveniles is reflected in the language used by the system. Although the various steps in the process of adult and juvenile courts are essentially the same, they are described by different terms. Author Thomas J. Bernard describes these differences:

> The flavor of the . . . juvenile court can be sensed by comparing some terms in that court with those in the criminal court. The terms in the criminal court convey a sense of fault, blame, accusation, guilt and punishment, while those in the juvenile court depict a sense of problems, needs, concern, helping, and caring.

Defendants in adult courts face an indictment—a written, formal accusation that a person has committed a crime.

Juvenile court has a petition—a written request for the court to look into the matter. The petition does not actually accuse the juvenile of committing a crime. Instead, it identifies the juvenile as possibly in need of the court's help.

Adult court has an arraignment, where the charges are formally read in the courtroom. Defendants plead guilty or not guilty. In juvenile court there is an intake hearing, at which the case is simply opened, and the court's jurisdiction over the juvenile is established. Although the petition alleges certain facts about the crime committed, the juvenile is not formally accused of the crime. Juvenile defendants do not plead guilty or not guilty. Instead, they admit to or deny the alleged facts of the case.

After the intake hearing, juveniles are given an adjudication hearing, which is the equivalent of a trial in the adult court. In the same way that a trial determines the guilt or innocence of an adult offender, the adjudication hearing determines whether the juvenile committed the offense or not. In an adjudication hearing, the case is heard by a judge rather than a jury.

Different punishment philosophies

Adult and juvenile courts operate under different philosophies when it comes to punishment. These philosophies mark the major differences between the adult and juvenile courts. A defendant convicted in adult court is sentenced or punished in proportion to the offense committed. The more serious the offense, the harsher the sentence or punishment. For many offenses, the adult court follows sentencing guidelines that set the length of punishment.

In juvenile court, the offender is not sentenced. Instead, the case has a disposition in which the juvenile's punishment is determined. Acting under the concept of *parens patriae*, the court determines a punishment that it considers to be in the best interest of the child rather than in proportion to the offense. In other words, the punishment is intended to redirect the offender toward a productive adult life rather than simply make him or her pay for the crime.

In this respect, it can be argued that the function of the juvenile court is not to punish offenders at all, but to help them change their behavior.

Discretionary power

The philosophy of *parens patriae* allows the juvenile court judge to review many options when determining juvenile punishment rather than following preset guidelines. The judge studies the young offender's background and selects a punishment aimed at rehabilitating the juvenile. Under this system, judges have a great deal of discretion, or flexibility, to choose a course they think is best.

Judges can send juveniles home with a stern lecture. They can place juveniles on probation, which requires them to make regular reports on their activities to an officer of the court. Judges can place juveniles in programs that offer chemical dependency treatment, counseling, discipline training, academic instruction, and other help. For serious offenses, judges can order juveniles to be held in a secure facility—the equivalent to adult jail or prison.

Acting in the juvenile's best interest does not necessarily mean that a juvenile receives light punishment. Young

This chart provides a simplified view, from left to right, of caseflow through the juvenile justice system.

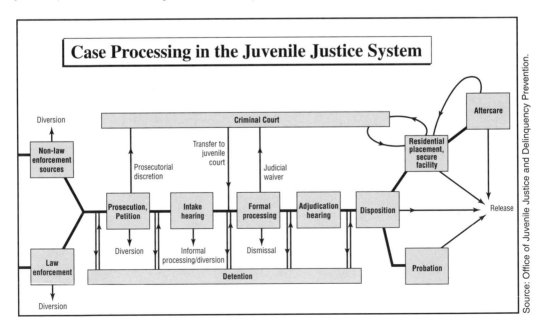

Source: Office of Juvenile Justice and Delinquency Prevention.

offenders can be confined until they reach the age of eighteen if the judge believes the juvenile will be at risk of committing crimes. So, a minor offense such as running away from home could stretch into long-term confinement, if the judge thinks this is the best option for helping the juvenile.

The discretionary power given to juvenile court judges can be viewed as essential to a system that deals exclusively with young people. Author Bernard describes why discretionary power benefits the juvenile justice process: "Because the problems they deal with often are very complex, it can be argued that juvenile justice officials need flexibility in their jobs. They need to have the freedom to respond to different cases differently, so that they can help as many children as much as possible."

As long as juvenile justice officials make good decisions about the juveniles that appear before them and administer punishments that rehabilitate juveniles, their discretionary power remains an asset to the system. But officials do not always make the right decisions. Often they make the wrong decisions and allow juveniles to return to the street where they will victimize again.

Failing the public

In the case of Max Brazley and Xavien Bendross, the two Florida youths who murdered the Dutch tourist, juvenile justice officials made the wrong decisions. Using their discretionary power, officials gave the pair light punishments for previous serious offenses and allowed them to remain on the street. Had the pair been confined to a detention center, it is possible that the crime may not have happened.

This and other similar cases in recent years have prompted harsh criticism of the juvenile justice system. For example, in an editorial appearing in the June 7, 1993, issue of *Forbes* magazine, publisher Steve Forbes echoed the sentiments of many Americans who felt the juvenile justice system was out of date and failing the public:

> States must radically overhaul their juvenile justice systems. The old notion that kiddie crime is an aberration that should be dealt with differently from adult crime is no longer

Henry Payne. Reprinted by permission of United Feature Syndicate, Inc.

tenable. A growing number of young people know that the current setup will treat their transgressions lightly, almost no matter how heinous the crime.

Critics say the juvenile justice system has failed to protect the public from violent juvenile offenders. Crime statistics show that young people today commit more crime and more violent crime than did juveniles of previous generations. This has led many to argue for an overhaul of the century-old juvenile justice system. Critics say the system cannot continue to give light punishments to juveniles who commit serious crimes. These critics worry that light punishments send a message to juveniles that the system will tolerate their behavior and that they can continue to commit offenses without fear of serious punishment.

Failing the juveniles

On the other end of the spectrum, some critics contend that the juvenile justice system is a failure because it does not protect the rights of juveniles. These critics argue that the discretionary power of the court has led to the abuse of juveniles' constitutional rights. In the adult system, for example, the accused must be given the opportunity to be represented by an attorney. During questioning and court appearances they do not have to say anything that might hurt their case. In the juvenile system offenders are often without legal counsel and frequently make statements that can be used against them in court. The U.S. Constitution guarantees the right of a speedy and public trial. However, juvenile court judges can order young offenders to be held without trial if such action is deemed to be within their best interests. For example, a judge could order a runaway to remain in confinement if the judge believed the juvenile would run away again.

In the 1960s and 1970s the U.S. Supreme Court heard several cases in which attorneys representing juveniles argued that the constitutional rights of their clients had been violated by the juvenile justice system. In a series of rulings the Supreme Court affirmed that juveniles had the same rights in the juvenile justice system as offenders in the adult system. Some critics argue, however, that the juvenile justice system frequently violates the constitutional rights of many juveniles despite the Supreme Court rulings. Many juveniles still go through the system without legal counsel. Many are talked into making statements that hurt their cases.

Juveniles are brought before a judge. Judges have more discretion and control over the sentencing of juveniles than they do over adults.

Critics also argue that especially harsh dispositions by the juvenile system can harden young offenders, turning them into career criminals. Harsh dispositions such as adult prison focus on punishment rather than rehabilitation. Juveniles sent to adult prisons are sometimes physically or sexually abused. Instead of learning new behavior, juveniles' old behavior is often reinforced. While protecting the general public, such dispositions do little or nothing to rehabilitate young offenders and so could be viewed as not being in the best interests of the child.

In the September 19, 1994, issue of *Time* magazine, Los Angeles County district attorney Gil Garcetti says that the existing juvenile justice system is beyond repair and presents his idea of what the system needs to accomplish. "We need to throw out our entire juvenile justice system," Garcetti says. "We should replace it with one that both protects society from violent juvenile criminals and efficiently rehabilitates youths who can be saved—and can differentiate between the two."

Fixing the juvenile justice system

Although no state has followed Garcetti's advice and dismantled its juvenile court system, officials throughout the nation are addressing some of the problems. Most efforts aim to increase public safety by keeping violent juvenile offenders off the streets.

One step officials have taken to achieve this goal is to charge violent juveniles as adults. A juvenile charged as an adult is tried in adult or criminal court rather than juvenile court. Juveniles tried and convicted as adults can receive longer, harsher punishments than if they were tried and convicted as juveniles. Longer sentences are intended to improve public safety by delaying or preventing return of violent juveniles to their communities.

Juveniles are transferred to adult court in several ways. Numerous states automatically transfer the most violent cases from juvenile to adult court. Prosecutors in other states have the authority to file specific juvenile cases in criminal court. Juvenile courts in forty-seven states can waive jurisdiction and transfer a juvenile offender to criminal court.

According to the National Juvenile Court Data Archive, an agency that collects data on the nation's juvenile court system, the number of juvenile cases transferred to criminal courts has increased greatly since 1985. This increase coincides with a rise in violent juvenile crime. In 1985, 7,200 juvenile cases were transferred to criminal court. By 1994 the number of juvenile cases moved to criminal court increased by 71 percent to 12,300. The seriousness of the offenses has also changed. Most cases transferred to criminal court in 1991 involved property offenses. In 1994 the majority of the cases involved personal offenses, or crimes committed against people. The increase in cases transferred from juvenile to adult court and the growing number of personal offenses transferred to adult court indicate that

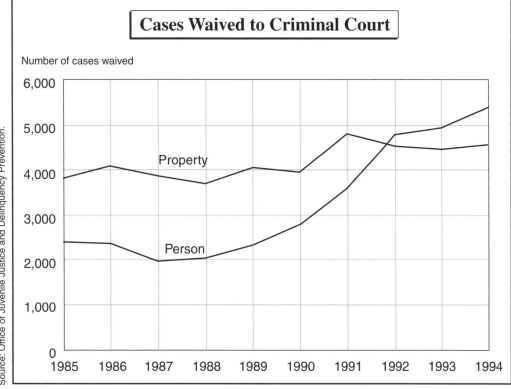

juvenile courts across the nation were attempting to deal more effectively with violent juvenile offenders.

New legislation

Many states have passed laws in recent years lowering the minimum age at which juveniles can be charged in criminal court. Offenders who are eighteen are automatically classified as adults. But increasingly, states are passing laws that allow juveniles as young as thirteen to be tried as adults when they commit homicide or other violent offenses. According to a National Governors' Association report, twenty-seven states passed such laws between 1992 and 1994.

Many states have also opened juvenile court hearings and juvenile court records to the public. Between 1992 and 1994, twenty-eight states changed their rules on the confidentiality of juvenile records, making information about juvenile offenders more accessible to the public. Some of those who support the opening of juvenile court hearings and records to the public say that closed proceedings violate a juvenile's right to a public trial as guaranteed by the Sixth Amendment to the U.S. Constitution.

Others believe that open juvenile proceedings would benefit the public by allowing citizens to gain more insight about how the system works. "It's all secret. Everything is behind closed doors," says Judge Heidi Schell, a Hennepin County, Minnesota, district court judge. "It [the public] virtually knows nothing and it cannot educate itself. I'm a very strong proponent of shining some light in our courtrooms."

Still others contend that open juvenile proceedings would force the courts to be more aware of young offenders who might commit repeat offenses. Schools, police, and the courts would be able to share their knowledge about a particular offender and use that information to craft more appropriate punishments. Experts say this might help the court system improve its ability to protect the general public and act in the best interests of the child.

Others believe that the juvenile courts should remain closed. Public attention would undermine the system's

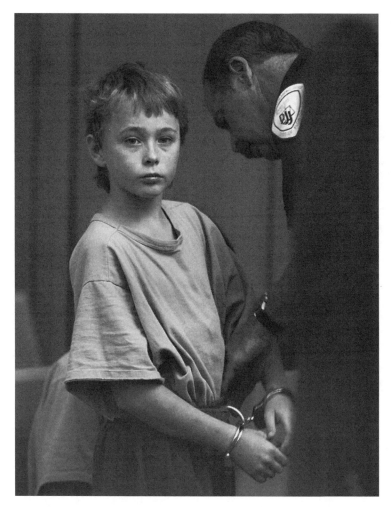

A ten-year-old boy appears in juvenile court for aiming a shotgun at a deputy. Many critics argue that the juvenile courts are unprepared to handle such violent youngsters.

goal of rehabilitation, these people argue. It would also disrupt the goal of reuniting young offenders with their families. Juveniles' willingness to report abuse and families' willingness to seek help might also be hampered by media attention if the court were opened to the public, experts argue.

In 1997 the U.S. Congress was considering laws that would aid states' efforts to toughen procedures for handling violent juvenile offenders. One proposal would allow prosecutors to decide whether juveniles arrested for violent crimes should be charged and tried as juveniles or adults. This decision currently rests with juvenile court judges

A young inmate peers out from the fence of a boot camp. Such camps are part of the movement toward stricter punishments for juveniles.

alone. Supporters of the proposal believe this change would lead to more juveniles being tried as adults.

Lawmakers are also considering the possibility of requiring states to adopt preset punishments for juvenile offenders, similar to the sentencing guidelines used in adult courts. If adopted, this measure would standardize punishments for juveniles, eliminating some of the discretionary power of the judges. Lawmakers are also considering provisions to open juvenile court records to the public.

The combined effect of these changes would recast the juvenile justice system to function more like the criminal system. For violent juveniles at least, the legal distinction between childhood and adulthood would be eliminated.

These changes worry child welfare advocates, who view the juvenile court's discretionary power as an asset. "Child-welfare advocates say [the proposed changes] would effectively dissolve the separate justice system for kids that dates back to 1899 when Chicago established the nation's first juvenile court," writes *Time* magazine reporter Richard Lacayo.

Whether all of these proposals become federal law remains to be seen. Whatever final form the law takes, it will most likely make the juvenile justice system tougher on violent juvenile offenders than it has been in the past.

An argument for success

Not everyone considers the juvenile justice system a failure. Juvenile justice expert Thomas J. Bernard observes that many juveniles who are not violent offenders are successfully processed by the juvenile justice system with little public interest. Bernard describes that system as more than a courtroom. The juvenile justice system begins with the police officers on the street. Many encounters between juveniles and police never result in an arrest and never reach the juvenile courts. Bernard also estimates that as few as nine cases out of six thousand police-juvenile encounters ever end up in criminal court. About sixty-four of these cases end with dispositions involving institutionalization in some kind of juvenile facility. Even if all of these cases are viewed as failures, Bernard says, the juvenile justice system still has a 96 percent success rate:

> If the juvenile justice system has such a remarkable success rate, then why does it have a widespread image of failure? The answer is that most studies of juvenile justice examine only the failures of the system and ignore the successes. Having excluded all the successful cases, the studies conclude that the system is a failure.

Even as debate about the success or failure of the juvenile justice system continues, many concerned people continue to search for new strategies that will help make the system more successful in accomplishing its mission. New punishment strategies for all kinds of juvenile offenders are being tested throughout the country. Juvenile justice authorities, lawmakers, and the general public are counting on these strategies to help end the wave of violent juvenile crime.

4

Punishing Juveniles

LIKE OTHER ASPECTS of the juvenile justice system, punishment strategies for juveniles are based on different criteria than those of the criminal justice system. Adults are usually sentenced in proportion to the severity of their offense. Their sentence is punishment for the crime committed. Juveniles are given a disposition, or punishment, based on what juvenile justice officials consider the best interests of the juvenile. Because juvenile punishment is based on the individual rather than the offense, preset guidelines are not used. Instead, justice officials select a disposition from a variety of options ranging from programs for first-time offenders guilty of minor crimes to the death penalty for offenders who commit the most violent crimes.

Although no set punishment guidelines exist for juvenile offenses, juvenile justice officials usually follow a similar strategy when they select a disposition. Their goal is to rehabilitate the juvenile offender so he or she can return to the community and lead a productive life. Young offenders who return to juvenile court are given harsher dispositions with each new appearance. Those who commit serious offenses and are judged to be a threat to the public safety are usually given the harshest dispositions.

The success of juvenile punishment is measured by whether the offender commits the same offense or other offenses after his or her punishment is complete. To determine which programs are the most successful, officials calculate the percentage of offenders who commit new offenses. The rate at which juveniles commit new offenses is known as the recidivism rate. The more successful programs have lower recidivism rates. The recidivism rate is usually expressed as the percentage of juveniles who commit new offenses. Sometimes, however, it is expressed in terms of the percentage of offenders who do not commit new offenses.

Diversionary programs

Most of the punishments ordered by the juvenile justice system are for minor offenses committed by first-time offenders. Minor offenses include truancy, drinking, and vandalism. First-time offenders who commit minor offenses

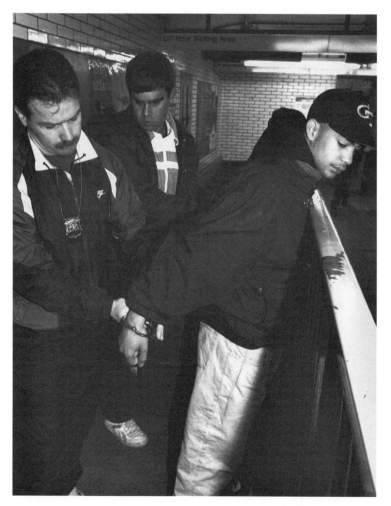

Undercover transit cops arrest a youth who attempted to ride the subway without paying the necessary fare. Most crimes committed by juveniles are nonviolent, minor offenses.

are usually enrolled in some type of diversionary program. The goal of a diversionary program is to correct the behavior that led to the offense by *diverting* the juvenile toward desirable behavior. The conditions of a diversion program vary from offender to offender. Juveniles involved in diversion programs normally remain at home during the time they are enrolled.

A 1996 report prepared by Ramsey County in Minnesota notes that a juvenile whose first offense is slashing tires would be placed in a diversion program. According to the report, a juvenile offender who commits such a crime could be required to undergo counseling to identify the reasons behind the offense. The juvenile might be required to perform a specified number of hours of community service working at tasks such as cleaning up trash or scraping graffiti from walls. The offender might also be required to apologize to the victim and reimburse that person for any damage.

Most first-time offenders do not commit additional offenses. According to one national estimate, 60 percent of juveniles never commit additional offenses after their first offense. Some agencies report even higher success rates. For example, the St. Paul (Minnesota) Youth Services Bureau, one of many public and private agencies that administer diversion programs for Ramsey County, found that 91 percent of the youths who participated in one of its diversion programs in 1996 had not returned to juvenile court in the six months after the original offense. Only 9 percent of the juveniles had committed new offenses that required new appearances in juvenile court.

Teen court

One of the more recent innovations in determining punishments for minor offenses committed by juveniles is teen court. One estimate indicates that more than two hundred teen courts operate in twenty-five states. Texas alone has thirty-five teen courts.

A teen court has an adult judge and a jury made up of teenagers. The jury listens to the case and determines the offender's punishment. Teen juries are often composed of former offenders who have already appeared before the court.

Teen courts generally hear cases referred from the juvenile court system. Referrals to teen court can also come from the district attorney's office, from schools, or from police. The defendant is usually a first-time offender who has already confessed to the offense and has agreed to abide by the teen court's decision. Typical cases handled by teen courts include truancy, shoplifting, drinking, smoking, and offensive behavior.

Effectiveness of teen court punishments

Punishments given by teen juries often involve some kind of restorative justice, that is, teens are required to correct what they did wrong. Experts who have observed teen courts say that teen juries look harshly on juveniles who do not take the court seriously. In Houston, Texas, for example, a sixteen-year-old girl was referred to the Family YMCA Teen Court after she admitted shoplifting a tube of lipstick from a department store counter. During the session the girl slouched in the witness stand and twirled her hair absentmindedly as if bored by the proceedings. The girl's seeming disinterest in the proceedings may have influenced her peers. She was sentenced to perform forty-eight hours of community service, attend an antitheft class, write a one-thousand-word essay, and serve on a teen court jury.

One reason for the popularity of teen courts is that they can devote time and attention to less serious cases that might get little notice in the crush of a crowded court schedule. "Everything we know would suggest kids who are dealt with very early on in the criminal justice system tend to do better than kids who penetrate further and further into the system," says Minnesota Corrections Commissioner Fred LaFluer. First-time offenders do not get much attention in courts overloaded with more serious crimes. Says LaFluer, "The juvenile justice system has tended to ignore that kid and say 'Come back when you're a really bad person.'"

Surveys indicate that teen courts have an influence on juvenile offenders. The November 18, 1996, issue of *Current Events* reported that only 25 percent of teens sentenced in a teen court are repeat offenders. Another survey published in the September 15, 1995, issue of *Scholastic Update* reported that fewer than 10 percent of offenders who go through teen court get arrested again. In contrast, the national average for repeat offenses by juveniles who do not go through teen court is 40 to 50 percent.

Not everyone is convinced of the benefits of teen courts. In some cases success rates of teen courts parallel success rates of other programs for first-time offenders. In other cases, adult judges have had to overrule teen juries that called for overly severe punishment. This is usually attributed to the inexperience and lack of maturity of young jurors.

Despite these lapses, teen juries remain a low-cost and often beneficial alternative for dealing with juveniles who have committed minor offenses. As Americans search for creative and cost-effective solutions to juvenile crime, the number of teen courts across the nation will most likely grow.

Repeat offenders

Repeat offenders are juveniles who commit crimes after their first offense. Although some repeat offenses are relatively minor, many others grow in seriousness. Whether the offenses are minor or serious, rehabilitation remains a primary goal of punishment for repeat offenders. Punishment often intensifies with each new offense. The Office of Juvenile Justice and Delinquency Prevention describes the basic goal of punishment for repeat offenders:

> An effective model for the treatment and rehabilitation of delinquent offenders must combine accountability and sanctions with increasingly intensive treatment and rehabilitation. The objective of graduated sanctions is to stop the juvenile's further slide into criminality by stimulating law-abiding behavior as early as possible.

"I REALIZE THIS IS JUVENILE COURT, YOUR HONOR, BUT WERE THE NOOGIES REALLY NECESSARY?"

Repeat offenders are often removed from their homes and temporarily placed in residential facilities to provide a better environment for rehabilitation. Residential facilities include foster homes, shelters, halfway houses, camps, ranches, and correctional facilities. They may be privately owned and operated or owned and operated by state and local governments. Authorities try to choose a facility that offers services that match the needs of the young offender. Alcohol and drug abusers, for example, might be placed in a facility that specializes in treating chemical dependency. Sex offenders may be sent to a facility that specializes in treating sex offenders.

Boys sent to the Safe Harbor Boys Home in Jacksonville, Florida, are in need of a stable home life. The "home," which is actually a refurbished U.S. Coast Guard tugboat, opened in the early 1980s when Doug and Robbie Smith were asked by local authorities to provide foster care for two youths.

Safe Harbor cares for boys between the ages of fifteen and eighteen. Most stay for up to three years. Residents are usually referred to the facility by the juvenile court system. Often the boys have had involvement with drugs. For example, Nathan, age sixteen, was sent to the home because of drug use and theft.

A probation officer talks to a teen who is in a juvenile detention center for prostitution. Many people believe juveniles deserve alternative punishments to prison.

Rehabilitation is the focus of Safe Harbor's program. Judge Mack Crenshaw of the Jacksonville juvenile court says the couple's program is very effective. It operates by "requiring kids to be responsible and imposing consequences when they aren't," Crenshaw says. The boys undergo a strict regimen which includes maintaining the tugboat, preparing meals, and restoring old boats donated to the facility. The boys are also required to perform community service such as picking up trash. Those who have not earned a high school diploma are required to continue their education.

Steve Barnes, a former resident who now works as a photographer, credited Safe Harbor with turning his life around: "I love [the Smiths] as much as my own parents. They saved my life." Most of the boys who have stayed at Safe Harbor have similar success stories. Of the 140 boys who have lived there, 126 stayed out of trouble in the first year after their release—which amounts to a recidivism rate of only 10 percent.

Boot camps

Boot camps are another type of residential facility for punishing repeat offenders. Boot camps place juveniles in a setting similar to facilities used for training military recruits. They aim to reshape behavior through military-style discipline and a demanding schedule of academics and physical exercise. Young offenders also learn to take responsibility for their actions and that their actions have consequences. Georgia and Oklahoma opened the first boot camps for juvenile offenders in 1983. By 1994, eight similar camps were operating around the country.

Boot camp programs are designed to show repeat offenders that criminal behavior is unacceptable. Steve Robinson, head of the Texas Youth Commission (TYC), which houses juveniles who have committed serious offenses, describes his agency's approach to young offenders:

> I was trained in the TYC way, which is to love kids, but our agency has got to be the ultimate hammer for kids who've been shooting the bird at the system and a hammer made of lightweight rubber won't do the trick. When a judge commits a kid to the TYC, I don't want the kid to say "So what?" I want him to say, "Oh, shit."

Boot camps have a strict routine. At the Manatee Boot Camp in Palmetto, Florida, for example, youths get up at 5 A.M. and spend several hours running and doing other physical exercise. The afternoon is spent in the classroom. Lights go out at 9 P.M. There is no television or radio. No profanity is allowed. Those who break the rules must do extra push-ups or write essays on what they did wrong.

Many young offenders have developed a new and healthy self-image as a result of the discipline, academic coursework, and lessons in responsibility offered by boot camps. Roy (not his real name) was sentenced to the Manatee Boot Camp when he was seventeen. Abandoned by his parents at the age of seven, he supported himself from the age of fourteen as a drug dealer. He was sent to boot camp after being arrested for attempted robbery. Roy describes the role boot camp played in his life:

It's changed me completely around. I used to think I had to be accepted by my friends. They'll bring you down just to bring you down to their standards. [Now] they have to come up to my standards. If they can't do that, I just can't be with them.

Roy's turnaround is one of many boot camp success stories. In its first year of operation only one of Manatee's fifty-nine graduates was arrested. Other camps have also had good results. In its May 9, 1994, issue, *U.S. News & World Report* notes that graduates of an Alabama boot camp were "arrested for 30 percent fewer felonies and 70 percent fewer misdemeanors than boys released from other correctional facilities."

Despite these encouraging results, many experts are withholding their endorsement of juvenile boot camps. Some experts say that more time and experience with boot camps will provide researchers with a more accurate picture of recidivism rates. Others question whether juveniles will lose the discipline and other lessons they

A juvenile boot camp in Virginia. Supporters believe such camps provide the structure and discipline that is missing from many juvenile offenders' lives.

New arrivals at a boot camp meet their drill instructors. Critics believe that the strict discipline and control juveniles experience at boot camps do not help them after they are released.

learned in camp after they leave. The return to troubled neighborhoods and old friends may undo all that was accomplished in boot camp. Critics point out that military boot camps, upon which juvenile camps are modeled, send their "graduates" on to serve a hitch in the armed forces. In that controlled environment, graduates are guaranteed a job and strict discipline and other lessons are maintained and reinforced.

University of Maryland researcher Doris Layton MacKenzie studied several boot camps for the U.S. Department of Justice. Some of her observations appear in the February 24, 1995, issue of *CQ Researcher:*

> There's something going on that may be positive, but it's not carrying through on the outside. They get back with the same crowd, they still can't get jobs and whatever problems they had before are still there. Those who were drug-involved return to their old community, return to their drug using friends and can't stay away from the problem.

Though their record is still unproven, some experts predict that boot camps will continue to rise in popularity. "Boot camps are so popular because it's perceived that we're finally doing something with these kids—not just putting them in a touchy-feely halfway house. It looks punitive, like the kids are really having to work for their

Boot camp inmates talk about their problems and concerns during a counseling session.

crimes," says Neil Kaltenecker, coordinator of juvenile boot camp development for Florida's Department of Health and Rehabilitative Services.

Secure facilities

Repeat juvenile offenders who commit serious or violent offenses and are judged a threat to public safety are sent to secure facilities. These facilities house young offenders convicted of crimes such as robbery, assault, or rape.

The Ethan Allan School for Boys near Wales, Wisconsin, has been described as the last stop before prison for juvenile offenders. The facility looks like a school, except that its perimeter is surrounded by chain-link fences and razor wire. At one end of the grounds is a maximum-security building with coils of razor wire around the roof and on top of the surrounding fence. A guard in a riot-proof central control booth monitors the building.

Young offenders sent to Ethan Allan have committed serious crimes such as battery, armed robbery, drug dealing, and sex offenses. Although offenders are sent to Ethan Allan because they are judged threats to the community, the emphasis of the school's program remains focused on rehabilitation. "In the adult system, prisoners are just there to do time—to pay a price," superintendent Jean Schneider says. "That's not true here. We're still trying to raise kids. We believe that people can change."

According to an Ethan Allan handbook, the school believes that "delinquency can be overcome through strength of will, positive human relationships, effective programs, education, and economic opportunity."

Offenders sent to Ethan Allan live in residential cottages. Like offenders in other residential facilities, they are required to attend school, go to therapy sessions, and work at campus jobs.

Ethan Allan's rehabilitation program works well for some repeat offenders. One seventeen-year-old inmate, interviewed in the February 1996 issue of the *Progressive*, explained how his experience at Ethan Allan changed his attitude. "This has helped me. You learn you can change. When I first came here, I went in the hole [maximum security] three or four times. But now I've got my anger under control. You learn there's consequences for your actions, and you get more freedoms as you progress."

A high recidivism rate

Lockup facilities like Ethan Allan do not have high success rates. One national study indicates that 52.6 percent of the juveniles released from this facility return to a juvenile lockup or go to prison within four years. Ethan Allen superintendent Jean Schneider blamed the high recidivism rate on a lack of follow-up after offenders leave the facility and return to their old neighborhoods. Juvenile justice budgets often do not include money for continued supervision and counseling after an offender is released. Without continued supervision and community support, offenders return to their old behavior.

But others place blame on the offenders themselves. Some juvenile justice experts argue that rehabilitation programs simply do not work for serious repeat offenders. Whether offenders willfully reject what they learn as soon as they are released or weaken and slide back into old behavior over a long period of time, they do not retain the lessons learned in rehabilitation programs. "I think it's fair to say that we do not know how to rehabilitate the serious repeat offenders," argues criminal justice expert James Q. Wilson, a professor at the University of California, Los Angeles. Because rehabilitation efforts fail, Wilson says, "the goal has to be: to protect society and make it clear to [young offenders] that society is not going to tolerate this behavior by ignoring it or winking at it."

Punishing juveniles as adults

As concerns about public safety grow, the nation has seen an emerging trend toward transferring juveniles who have committed violent offenses such as rape, aggravated assault, and homicide to criminal court and imposing adult punishments upon them. This trend is described by authors Mike Males and Fay Docuyanan in the February 1996 issue of the *Progressive*.

> Today, state after state is imposing harsher penalties on juveniles who run afoul of the law. . . . Rehabilitation and reintegration into the community are concepts that have already fallen out of fashion for adult criminals. Now they are fast becoming passé for juveniles, as well. Instead of prevention and rehabilitation programs, more prisons are being built to warehouse juveniles along with adults.

To date, only a small percentage of juvenile offenders have been affected by this trend. In Ramsey County, Minnesota, for example, the juvenile justice system transferred thirty-two juveniles to adult court in 1995. That figure was more than double the fourteen juveniles certified as adults in 1992. Nevertheless, the thirty-two juveniles certified as adults in 1995 represented less than one-half of 1 percent of the total number of juvenile cases processed by the county that year.

Transfer of a juvenile to adult court does not automatically guarantee that the young offender will be sent to an adult prison. Often judges and juries hesitate to send a juvenile to an adult prison, fearing the environment is too harsh. Instead, juveniles are returned to juvenile facilities or are given little or no punishment. According to California statistics only 10 to 12 percent of juveniles who are transferred to criminal court spend any time in adult prison.

Some juvenile justice experts, however, worry about the trend toward certifying more juveniles as adults. Ira M. Schwartz, dean of the University of Pennsylvania's School of Social Work, believes that punishing juveniles as adults could have disastrous effects on society because juveniles could not be rehabilitated in adult prisons. Often, juvenile offenders are physically or sexually abused by adult inmates. Such experiences deepen rather than alter antisocial attitudes and behavior. Juvenile offenders housed in adult prisons would become career criminals, Schwartz believes. The practice "gives the community a false sense of public protection. It may be good politics, but it's not very good public policy," Schwartz says.

Some states have sought to strike a balance between harsher, longer punishments that would keep violent juveniles off the streets and traditional efforts to rehabilitate them. Colorado, for example, has developed a program that gives longer sentences to violent juvenile offenders, housing them in specially created institutions that include rehabilitation programs. Minnesota took a different approach to sharpen consequences for juvenile offenders. As of 1995, serious juvenile offenders can be given two sentences at once—one in juvenile court and another in adult court. If the young offender fails to meet all requirements imposed

A juvenile offender and his parole officer stand before a judge. Many people contend that violent juveniles should receive harsh punishments, including the death penalty.

by the juvenile court or commits a new offense before the age of twenty-one, the adult sentence goes into effect.

The death penalty

Perhaps the most controversial issue in punishing juveniles is whether the death penalty is an appropriate punishment for violent young offenders. The United States is one of only a half-dozen countries in the world that allow the death penalty for offenders under the age of eighteen. Nine individuals who committed their crimes as juveniles have been executed in the United States since 1973.

In 1989, the Supreme Court upheld the right of states to impose the death penalty on juveniles in the case of *Stanford v. Kentucky*. In 1981, seventeen-year-old Kevin Stanford and an accomplice raped, sodomized, and murdered Baerbel Poore. The murder took place in Jefferson County, Kentucky, during a robbery of the gas station where the victim worked as an attendant. After his arrest, Stanford told police, "I had to shoot her [since] she lived next door to me and she would recognize me. . . . I guess we could have tied her up or something or beat [her up] and [told] her if she tells, we would kill her."

A jury convicted Stanford of first-degree murder. The judge sentenced him to death. Stanford appealed the case, but eight years after the crime was committed the U.S. Supreme Court upheld the judge's sentence. Stanford remained on Death Row as of June 30, 1996.

The decision to impose the death penalty is made by each state. Today, thirteen states allow the death penalty for eighteen-year-olds, four states allow the death penalty for seventeen-year-olds, and twenty-one states allow the death penalty for sixteen-year-olds. Twelve states have no legal age limit or do not allow the death penalty.

The case of Joseph Hudgins

Forty-seven inmates on Death Row in late 1996 committed their offenses as juveniles, a 39 percent increase over 1983. One of them is Joseph Hudgins of South Carolina, who was arrested for murder at the age of seventeen. On December 6, 1992, Hudgins, along with another juvenile named Terry Cheek, stole a pest exterminator's truck. They parked it on a back road. A deputy sheriff named Chris Taylor stopped to investigate. Apparently he ushered the two boys into the back of the patrol car because it was raining. A motorist passed by, returned five minutes later, and spotted Taylor lying in the roadway. He had been shot in the face. He died a short time later.

Hudgins eventually confessed to the killing. Before his trial started, however, the youth's lawyers reenacted the crime in a motel parking lot. The reenactment convinced them that Hudgins could not have killed Taylor.

Hudgins finally admitted that he had agreed to "take the rap" because, as the younger of the two, he would get a lighter sentence. Cheek pleaded guilty to a lesser crime.

Despite the defense team's argument that Hudgins was not the killer, a jury convicted him based on his confession. In a second phase of the trial jurors considered whether he should receive the death sentence. The prosecutor argued against preferential treatment of Joseph Hudgins simply because he was a juvenile. His argument is quoted in the October 5, 1995, issue of *Rolling Stone* magazine.

> He had four weapons that he took with him. Those bolt cutters, this ski mask, that gun and one more that's not so readily apparent. And that is the shield of youth. Should he receive extra credit because he was able to kill somebody at a younger age than a lot of other people are when they kill somebody?

The jurors agreed with the prosecutor's argument. On July 23, 1993, Joseph Hudgins was sentenced to death in South Carolina for his role in the murder of the deputy sheriff.

Writing about Hudgins's case in *Rolling Stone*, Tina Rosenberg argues that the same characteristics that make juveniles prone to commit violent acts are reasons to question whether the death penalty is a suitable punishment for them:

> Some of the very qualities that make juvenile criminals most terrifying—their impulsiveness, a tendency to fall under the sway of others and a need to prove their toughness to the group—raise questions about their suitability for a punishment that the law reserves for a small group of the most morally culpable killers. Minors are thought to be too immature to sit on a jury, vote, buy beer or watch an X-rated movie, yet they are considered responsible enough to pay for their crimes with their lives.

As of March 1997, Joseph Hudgins remained on South Carolina's Death Row. The issue of whether the death penalty is appropriate for juvenile offenders may take on increased importance if the predicted violent juvenile crime wave materializes. One study found that use of the death penalty for juveniles has not increased dramatically since violent juvenile crime began rising in the mid-1980s.

The case of Azikiwe Kambule

However, opponents of the death penalty fear that the courts may turn to this extreme punishment more often in the future. Their concerns were realized in February 1997 when a prosecutor sought the death penalty for Azikiwe Kambule, a seventeen-year-old Jackson, Mississippi, youth who admitted his involvement in the murder of thirty-one-year-old Pamela McGill. On January 25, 1996, Kambule and twenty-one-year-old Santonio Berry kidnapped McGill and drove to a wooded area. While Kambule waited in the car, Berry forced McGill into the woods and shot her.

After the two were arrested, Berry agreed to plead guilty and testify against Kambule in exchange for a life sentence without parole. Just before the case went to trial, however, a judge ruled that the death penalty was inappropriate in Kambule's case because it would condemn him to a harsher punishment than the man who actually

did the shooting. Even though the judge ultimately ruled that the death penalty was inappropriate in this case, opponents fear that more prosecutors will seek the death penalty.

Despite a trend toward stiffer punishment designed to protect the public from violent juvenile offenders, rehabilitation remains a primary focus of punishment programs administered by the juvenile justice system. But the overall success of rehabilitation as a punishment strategy remains inconclusive. Although intervention and rehabilitation seem to influence many first-time juvenile offenders, statistics indicate that rehabilitation fails to influence repeat offenders. The absence of conclusive results has focused attention on preventing juvenile crime.

5

Preventing Juvenile Crime

JUST AS MANY strategies are used to punish juvenile offenders, a wide variety of strategies have been developed to prevent juveniles from becoming offenders. In general, prevention measures follow one of two strategies. One strategy is to set limits or establish boundaries and guidelines for juveniles. Another strategy is to offer juveniles alternative activities to street life, or to work toward improving the lives of poor and disadvantaged children. Communities throughout the nation combine these prevention strategies in their efforts to combat juvenile crime.

Curfews

An increasing number of cities have turned to curfews to help reduce juvenile crime. A curfew is a predesignated time by which all juveniles must be off the streets and in their homes. The purpose of a curfew is to prevent juveniles from being out at night when many crimes are committed. Authorities believe that curfews reduce crime committed by juveniles and protect them from becoming crime victims.

Curfew times differ from city to city. In New Orleans, juveniles under the age of eighteen must be in their homes by 8 P.M. on weeknights and by 11 P.M. on Friday and Saturday nights. In other cities curfews go into effect between 10 P.M. and midnight and continue until the next morning.

A sign in Austin, Texas, proclaims a 10 P.M. curfew for juveniles. Cities that have enacted such curfews have seen a sharp decrease in juvenile crime.

A 1995 survey by the National Conference of Mayors indicated that the number of youth curfews established by cities around the country increased by 45 percent between 1990 and 1995. Of 387 cities responding to the survey, at least 270 had established curfews.

Although no national data about the success of curfews exists, individual cities have reported reduced juvenile crime rates during the restricted hours. Among cities with curfews, 56 percent rated their curfews as somewhat or very effective while only 14 percent considered them ineffective. In New Orleans the curfew decreased crime 27 percent during restricted hours. In Washington, D.C., the metropolitan police department reports felony juvenile arrests during curfew hours declined 34 percent between July 16 and September 30, 1995, when compared with the same period in 1994, when no curfew was in effect.

Despite their popularity, curfews have also been criticized by numerous groups. No studies conclusively show that curfews reduce crime rates. While they may not be harmful, some critics argue, curfews are ineffective because they do not keep potential troublemakers off the streets. Young people who are intent on causing trouble will simply ignore curfew hours, or move their activities to backyards or other areas exempt from police jurisdiction. Since most curfews have exceptions for juveniles attending school activities or working at late-night jobs, street-smart juveniles simply lie when stopped by police. Barry Krisberg, executive director of the National Council on Crime and Delinquency, says, "There are all sorts of things you can say to legally prohibit a police officer from taking you into custody. The only kids who get caught are the poor schnooks who don't know what they're doing." Some critics argue that curfews are racist, claiming some police pick up minority juveniles on curfew violations more often than they pick up white juveniles.

The American Civil Liberties Union (ACLU), an advocacy organization for civil rights, believes that curfews violate juveniles' constitutional rights of peaceful assembly

and free speech. The ACLU has challenged the constitutionality of curfews in several cities. For example, in Miami, Florida, the ACLU successfully argued that the city's curfew violated juveniles' constitutional rights of peaceful assembly and free speech, convincing a judge to overturn the curfew. However, the ACLU was unable to convince the court to overturn the curfew in Dallas, Texas. Cities have responded to ACLU challenges by attempting to draft curfew ordinances that accomplish their goal without violating juveniles' rights.

Finally, some parents and teens dislike curfews, claiming that they punish all teens for the crimes committed by only a minority of juveniles. Parents and teens in some cities complain that curfews can interfere with legitimate late-night errands or even household chores like walking the dog. Fifteen-year-old Jessica Levi expresses her frustration with the Washington, D.C., curfew in the September 15, 1995, issue of *Scholastic Update*. "It is totally and completely wrong to punish all of the teenagers when only a small percentage are the really guilty ones."

School uniforms

Another strategy for preventing juvenile crime is the adoption of school uniforms. School officials like uniforms for various reasons. A uniform eliminates from campus the expensive brand-name jackets, athletic shoes, and other items that are frequently the target of thefts. Theft has become a major problem on some campuses; some students have even been injured during thefts of jackets or shoes.

Schools in cities with gang problems like uniforms for another reason. Uniform requirements at schools prevent students from wearing "colors"—items or colors that identify gang membership. School administrators believe that if colors are eliminated from schools, fewer confrontations will break out between members of rival gangs.

Long Beach, California, launched the nation's first districtwide experiment with school uniforms in 1994. The policy, which required approval of two-thirds of local parents, applied to elementary and middle schools. Parents liked the idea. "It's a very good idea," says parent James Sutton. "It helps to prevent a lot of gang activity for kids because they aren't paying attention to what the other kids are wearing. They are learning, instead."

District officials noticed a difference in crime rates within the schools soon after the uniform rule went into effect. According to the *CQ Researcher* for March 15, 1996,

> Within a year of its implementation, school-based crime and violence plummeted in Long Beach. Assault and battery cases declined 34 percent, fighting 51 percent, drug cases 69

President Clinton and a student pose with the uniforms implemented by the Long Beach, California, school district. Officials credit the uniforms with drastically reducing crime rates at the city's schools.

percent and sex offenses 74 percent. . . . Moreover, attendance rates and test scores are up in Long Beach, overall crime in the district has plunged 36 percent and suspensions are down 32 percent.

School districts that require uniforms can now be found in California, Georgia, Florida, Louisiana, Maryland, New York, Virginia, Washington, and Washington, D.C.

Not all schools report success with uniforms. In Garden Grove, California, a voluntary school-uniform program was enacted in 1995. About half of the students initially wore the uniforms, but the numbers dwindled. By the end of 1995, fewer than one-third of the students were still wearing uniforms. Officials found that uniforms had little effect on school discipline.

The difference between the Long Beach and Garden Grove programs was the fact that the Long Beach policy was mandatory, which meant that students had to follow it. But making school uniforms mandatory raises constitutional issues. The U.S. Supreme Court ruled in 1969 that the First Amendment protects the right to individual dress. The American Civil Liberties Union has argued that ordering students to wear school uniforms violates students' First Amendment right of freedom of expression. So far, however, no court has ruled against school uniforms. In Phoenix, Arizona, for example, the ACLU backed two students who sued the school district over dress requirements. The court ruled against the students, saying it was not the court's responsibility to second-guess the decision of the school board in implementing a mandatory dress policy.

Parental responsibility

Experts have long believed that strong parental involvement is the key to preventing a young person from drifting toward criminal behavior. Some parents, however, are unwilling or unable to control the behavior of their children. Laws have existed for years that make it possible for parents to be held financially responsible for crimes committed by their children. But in recent years,

Two parents sit in a Michigan courtroom on trial under a law that holds them legally responsible for the delinquent actions of their son. Many parents argue that they cannot control their teens and should not be held responsible for their behavior.

communities have adopted ordinances that make parents' failure to supervise their children a crime.

Silverton, Oregon, pioneered the parental responsibility concept in 1995. The city council hoped to stem a wave of minor crimes committed by juveniles by allowing judges to levy fines of up to one thousand dollars against parents who had failed to adequately supervise their children. The council also gave judges the power to order parents to take parenting classes. The ordinance was not intended as punishment, Silverton officials said. Rather, it sought to force parents to take a stronger role in their children's lives.

As of March 1996, eleven parents had been cited under the Silverton ordinance. Their children's offenses included beer drinking, smoking, marijuana use, and shoplifting. According to Silverton officials, the city's juvenile crime rate declined by 55 percent in the first nine months after the ordinance took effect. Officials attributed the decrease to better supervision by parents. The Silverton law was later adopted statewide.

Parental responsibility ordinances are one of the more controversial strategies for preventing juvenile crime. They raise a fundamental question about who is responsible for juvenile crime—the juvenile who commits the crime or the parents.

Parents argue that they cannot supervise their children every minute of the day. "It was like a blow," says parent Sylvia Whitney. Whitney was charged with failing to supervise her fifteen-year-old son Scott, after he was picked up for drinking alcohol. Whitney was fined and ordered to attend parenting classes. Whitney describes her feelings in the March 1996 issue of *Good Housekeeping*. At first she thought, "I must be a terrible parent. But then I thought about it and started to get mad. You do everything you can to raise your kids well, but you can't supervise them twenty-four hours a day."

Scott Whitney believes the blame for his actions is misplaced. "I don't think it's my parents' fault. You do the crime, you do the time. That's the way I think it should be."

A question of constitutionality

Detractors of ordinances like the one in Silverton assert that it is unconstitutional to hold parents responsible for crimes they did not commit. "If you want to charge someone with a crime, you have to prove that she herself did something wrong," says attorney Jossi Davidson. Davidson represented one Silverton parent who challenged the ordinance. That parent, Anita Beck, faced a charge of failing to supervise her fifteen-year-old son after he was caught shoplifting a bottle of perfume. The judge who heard Beck's case ruled that Beck was not guilty because she had tried to supervise her son.

Concern about the constitutionality of parental responsibility ordinances has caused some cities to reject them. Farmington, Minnesota, for example, considered a parental responsibility ordinance in 1996. After much debate, city officials rejected the proposed ordinance because they doubted it could withstand a constitutional challenge.

Cutting off the supply of guns

Removing guns from the community is another strategy officials are using to reduce juvenile crime. Firearms are used in three out of four homicides committed by juveniles nationwide. A Justice Department survey found that most

A gang member shows off his gun. Many law enforcement officers believe that removing guns from the hands of juveniles is the key to preventing the violent crimes they commit.

of the 835 juvenile inmates in six high-security institutions had used guns in crimes ranging from violent assault to homicide. Juvenile justice authorities see removing guns from the community as one of the best ways to slow the trend of violent juvenile crime.

The impact of cutting off the supply of guns was demonstrated in Boston, Massachusetts, in the early 1990s. Boston police traced handguns sold to gang members, including some juveniles, to one individual in Mississippi. Investigators found that a Boston native attending Mississippi State University was buying guns in Mississippi and selling them at home in Boston on weekends.

The student was convicted in U.S. district court on federal gun trafficking charges. Police reported ninety-one shootings in the neighborhood in the five months before his arrest and twenty shootings in the five months after his arrest. Boston officials believe that turning off this source of guns reduced the number of shootings.

Officials are working to remove weapons from communities in several ways. Many cities have organized gun buy-back programs in which a city pays money for weapons turned in by residents. Such programs accept weapons from adults and juveniles alike. Any weapon turned in, officials believe, is one less weapon that could fall into the hands of a juvenile. In Omaha, Nebraska, for example, an organization called MAD DADS staged gun buy-back programs in 1992 and 1993 that netted 1,712 guns. Among the many guns turned in by juveniles was a 12-gauge shotgun owned by Doug, the subject of a *Time* cover story on juveniles and guns.

Lawmakers have toughened up laws to prevent the legal sale of firearms to juveniles. A federal law passed in 1994 prohibited the sale of guns to juveniles by licensed gun dealers. Individual states have also revised old laws or passed new ones banning adults from selling or giving guns to juveniles or prohibiting juveniles under eighteen from possessing firearms.

Officials are also trying to stop the illegal sale of guns to juveniles. Officials believe that many of the guns juveniles use are obtained illegally. Illegal weapons "pass along the links of the chain until they land in the hands of adolescents," says Raymond W. Kelly, undersecretary of law enforcement at the Treasury Department. Authorities believe that only a small percentage of registered dealers traffic in illegal guns. One estimate suggested that as few as 1 percent of the 160,000 registered gun dealers are responsible for 51 percent of all the guns used in crime. Research has indicated that juvenile offenders prefer new guns to older guns. Thus officials believe that many juveniles buy guns from dealers illegally, or have an adult buy the gun for them. If dealers who traffic in illegal sales can be identified, authorities reason, the supply of guns to juveniles can be significantly reduced.

Gun tracking

In the summer of 1996 President Bill Clinton announced the creation of a federal computer system to trace the origins of guns seized from juveniles who commit a crime. Seventeen cities began sending information on such guns to a data system managed by the Bureau of Alcohol, Tobacco and Firearms. Using various documents and the weapon's serial number, officials trace the weapon to the original seller.

In the initiative's first year of operation, law enforcement agencies tracked thirty-seven thousand guns used in crimes back to their sources—almost twice as many as the year before, according to Treasury Department statistics. Treasury officials estimate that four out of every ten guns seized were originally sold to juveniles. Ultimately, authorities hope they will be able to prosecute dealers who illegally sell firearms to juveniles.

It will be some time before officials know whether they have broken the chain that places guns in the hands of adolescents. Authorities will have to monitor the number of juvenile crimes committed with guns in participating cities in order to evaluate the program's success.

Eleven more cities joined the gun-tracking program in summer 1997. Among them is Minneapolis, Minnesota, a city that has experienced a sharp rise in homicides in recent years. Between January 1994 and May 1997, juveniles were responsible for 12 percent of that city's homicides. Mayor Sharon Sayles-Belton believes the tracking program will make a difference in her city. "This [program] will boost our efforts to keep guns out of the hands of children and reduce violent juvenile crime."

Controlling gangs

Street gangs have been linked to the illegal drug industry and to the nation's homicide rate. In 1994, for example, 43 percent of all homicides committed nationwide were believed to be gang related. Because many gang members are juveniles, cities around the country are working to control gangs to prevent juvenile crime.

One city that successfully broke up its gangs is Charleston, South Carolina. When Rueben Greenberg became police chief in 1992, he made his views about juvenile crime known and organized a campaign to break up the city's gangs. "The quicker kids learn there are limits, the better off everyone is," Greenberg told an interviewer. Part of the campaign was directed at graffiti. All graffiti reported by 10 A.M. was eliminated by 5 P.M. the same day, painted over by jail prisoners and police officers. "The presence of graffiti means it's their turf," Greenberg said. "The absence of graffiti means it's ours."

Greenberg and the police force also went after gang members themselves, issuing citations for minor traffic offenses. "We'd nail them for everything we could, rolling

A member of the gang squad in Detroit helps with an arrest. Some cities implement such squads to intimidate and harass gangs into stopping their activities.

past stop signs, burned-out lights over their license plates, jaywalking, throwing down cigarette butts."

Skeptics viewed such measures as ineffective. But Greenberg stuck to his plan. Arrested gang members were fingerprinted, put through background checks, and photographed for police files.

"People thought we were crazy for citing drug dealers for littering, but since they never paid their citations, after about six weeks we'd have warrants on them so we could arrest them pretty much at will," Greenberg said. That allowed police to search gang members' vehicles. If they found drugs or guns, they confiscated the gang member's car. "We literally ate them alive with minor violations," Greenberg said. The harassing tactics worked. Gang members were either incarcerated through convictions on drug or gun offenses, or they left the community. Over a period of time such tactics virtually eliminated gangs from the city.

GREAT

All cities with gang problems employ some type of program to keep juveniles from joining gangs. A program developed in 1991 by the Phoenix Police Department and the Bureau of Alcohol, Tobacco and Firearms has been adopted by an estimated eight hundred communities nationwide. GREAT, which stands for Gang Resistance, Education, and Training, is a nine-week course taught by uniformed police officers.

The course targets seventh-grade students because they are considered most at risk of getting involved in criminal activity. GREAT officials have also developed a curriculum for third- and fourth-grade students because juvenile violence is now being reported at a younger age.

The course consists of nine one-hour sessions focusing on topics such as prejudice, cultural sensitivity, conflict resolution, and goal setting. A follow-up summer program consists of classroom and extracurricular activities to help children develop social skills and build self-esteem.

Because GREAT is a fairly new program, it remains unknown whether it has been successful in reducing gang membership. A five-year study now in progress should be completed before the year 2000. A preliminary study in one community indicated that gang membership declined by 15 percent after the GREAT program began. Some communities have criticized the program because it is expensive to implement. Others dislike it because it takes police officers off the streets, where they are much in need.

Support programs

Support programs seek to prevent juvenile crime by providing a more structured environment for juveniles. Many different types of support programs exist. Some provide entertainment activities to divert juveniles from the streets. Others provide health services and education for young children or teach adults parenting skills so they will raise healthier children.

Two boys participate in a recreational program at their local church. The program, aimed at deterring juvenile crime, includes activities such as conflict mediation and basketball.

Among the most successful support programs are those that provide recreational activities for young people. Many communities offer such programs in neighborhood centers and parks to keep children busy and off the streets. Phoenix, Arizona, received financial support for its programs from an unusual source: the Arizona Supreme Court. Departing from its traditional judicial role, the court decided to get involved in crime prevention. In 1991 and 1993 the court funded recreation programs in Phoenix. In 1993 the Arizona Supreme Court gave $863,000 to the Phoenix Parks, Recreation, and Library Department. City government added another $837,000 to that amount.

"Constructive program alternatives"

The parks department spent the money on five different programs. One was the Juvenile Curfew Youth Counseling program, which offered counseling to youths who violated curfew. During August 1993, 467 youths were picked up for curfew violations. Of those, 105 were contacted by the youth counselor, and 80 took advantage of the offered services.

A second program funded by the grants, known as Kool Kids, provided free access to nine Phoenix swimming pools for 82,122 youths up to age seventeen. In addition, some of the city's parks and recreation centers offered evening and weekend programs. Officials estimated that up to 231,405 juveniles took part in this program. The City Streets Outreach program, which sponsored late-night teen sports, teen councils, athletic tournaments, and other services also received money. Finally, schools in neighborhoods with gang problems offered after-hours recreational programs.

The results of the Phoenix programs were encouraging. Phoenix Police Department statistics for July and August 1991, 1992, and 1993 show a reduction in crime calls by as much as 52 percent in areas with expanded recreational programs. This reduction came at a time when statistics nationwide showed that juvenile crime was on the rise.

Phoenix parks department director Jim Colley praised his city's program and called on other parks departments around the nation to offer similar programs.

> It made the streets of Phoenix safer by giving them some constructive program alternatives. . . . The challenge to the parks and recreations profession is to take the initiative in putting together similar programs to combat juvenile crime and delinquency. While we are not the only solution, parks and recreation is a very valuable part of the chain.

Head Start

Some support programs attempt to improve the lives of poor and disadvantaged children through education and training. It is hoped that by offering educational opportunities to these children at a young age, they will be more likely to avoid a life of crime and dependency on government resources. Many organizations, including government, private institutions, churches, clubs, and charities

Children play at a Head Start program. Supporters of Head Start believe that early education programs will later deter these children from becoming criminals.

Children in Head Start listen attentively to their teacher. The federal government funds the program to help prepare poor children for school and promote their success.

sponsor such programs. One of the most well known support programs is Head Start, a federal government program that helps young children from disadvantaged families get a "head start" in life. The program provides preschool instruction, home visits, and social services. Past studies have shown that children who participate in Head Start are generally better off than their peers. They finish high school and hold jobs at higher rates and are less likely to end up on welfare than peers who do not take part in Head Start.

The federal government has funded Head Start since it began in 1965 based on the belief that the program helps the young children avoid the pitfalls of crime and leads to life as a successful adult. Among the parents who have benefited from Head Start is Debra Lloyd-Kemp, a resident of Portland, Oregon. Lloyd-Kemp describes the benefits she and her family received from Head Start while she was going through a divorce and on welfare. Her young son Joshua had trouble talking and needed speech therapy.

> Head Start offered the only preschool program with free speech therapy. Head Start taught Josh how to talk. It also provided services for the whole family, not just the child. . . . [It] taught me supportive parenting skills, hands-on, respectful nurturing, treating babies as capable beings, how to talk to them and step by step, how to tell them what you are going to do.

Supporters argue that the training Joshua and his mother received will make Joshua a more successful individual who is less likely to participate in criminal behavior in the future. This crime prevention, Head Start supporters contend, will save the government money in the long run.

Critics of Head Start argue that the long-term savings claimed by supporters are exaggerated, because what the "head start" children receive does not remain with them as they grow older. An analysis conducted in 1985 by the U.S. Department of Health and Human Services, for example, concluded that "Children enrolled in Head Start enjoy significant immediate gains in cognitive test scores, socioemotional test scores, and health status. In the long run, cognitive and socioemotional test scores of former Head Start students do not remain superior to those of disadvantaged children who did not attend Head Start."

Head Start continues to be one of the most popular support programs for young children. In 1994 President Clinton signed a bill extending Head Start into 1998. Funds allocated for the fiscal year 1995 totaled $4 billion, an amount expected to reach seven hundred thousand children.

Epilogue

Because juvenile crime has many causes, its reduction will probably require a combined effort of large and small programs. Many of these programs are already under way, and the causes of juvenile crime are under attack from many directions. Some experts argue, however, that violent juvenile crime will not be reduced by punishment and prevention strategies alone. These must be accompanied by changes in society.

More and more officials regard violent juvenile behavior as a by-product of society's tolerance of violence. Author Deborah Prothrow-Stith believes that violence can be "unlearned" by our culture. To combat violence in society, Prothrow-Stith suggests that violence be "addressed as a gross assault on the public health."

Police arrest suspected gang members. Some experts credit the rise in juvenile crime, including gang violence, to an increased tolerance and acceptance of violence by society.

Recognizing violence as a public health problem, she says, will help focus the nation's attention on the issue. Capturing the nation's attention is the first step in changing societal attitudes. Constant repetition of the message that violence hurts our society could change tolerant attitudes toward violence. Prothrow-Stith writes:

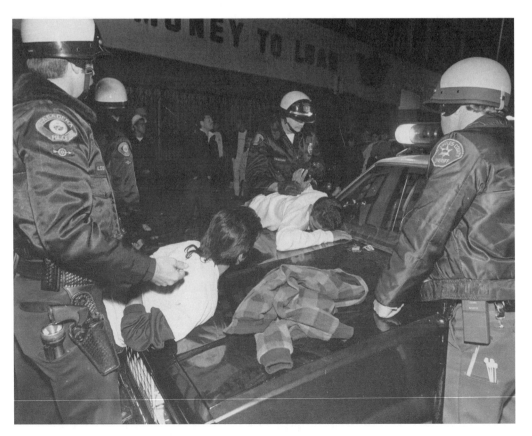

Over time, employing an array of interventions, the public health approach can change people's attitudes, and in the long run, their destructive behavior. We have done this with cigarettes. Following a massive twenty-year public health campaign the incidence of smoking has decreased by 30 percent. We have done this with drunk driving. Americans no longer believe it is all right to drive when intoxicated or allow a friend to drive home when intoxicated. We have done this with exercise and diet, convincing millions of Americans to adopt more healthful lifestyles in order to reduce their risk of heart disease and stroke. I believe that we can do the same thing for violence.

By demanding changes in the juvenile justice system, by toughening punishments, and by devising prevention strategies, our society appears to already be changing its attitude about violence and violent juvenile offenders.

Organizations
to Contact

American Civil Liberties Union (ACLU)
125 Broad St., 18th Floor
New York, NY 10004-2400
(212) 549-2500
(800) 775-ACLU (publications)
e-mail: aclu@aclu.org
Internet: http://www.aclu.org

The ACLU is a national organization that works to defend Americans' civil rights as guaranteed by the U.S. Constitution. It opposes curfew laws for juveniles and others and seeks to protect the public-assembly rights of gang members or people associated with gangs.

**California Youth Authority Gang Violence
Reduction Policy**
2445 Mariondale Ave., Suite 202
Los Angeles, CA 90032-3516
(213) 227-4114
fax: (213) 227-5169

Operated by state parole agents, the project's goal is to mediate feuds among gangs in East Los Angeles. Its activities include developing job opportunities for former gang members, removing graffiti, and establishing parent groups. The project publishes a directory of organizations concerned with gangs as well as various pamphlets, including *Facts on Gangs* and *A Parent's Guide to Children's Problems*.

Educational Fund to End Handgun Violence
100 Maryland Ave., Suite 402
Washington, DC 20002
(202) 544-7214
fax: (202) 544-7213
e-mail: edfund@aol.com
Internet: http://www.gunfree.org

The fund helps to educate the public about handgun violence in the United States and examines how such violence affects children in particular. The fund participates in the development of educational materials and programs to help persuade teenagers not to carry guns, and it examines the impact of handguns on public health. Its publications include the booklet *Kids and Guns: A National Disgrace* and the quarterly newsletters *Assault Weapon and Accessories in America* and *Firearms Litigation Reporter*.

Juvenile Justice Clearinghouse (JJC)
PO Box 6000
Rockville, MD 20849-6000
(800) 638-8736
fax: (301) 251-5212
e-mail: askncjrs@ncjrs.org
Internet: http://www.ncjrs.org/ojjhome.htm

The Juvenile Justice Clearinghouse, a service of the Office of Juvenile Justice and Delinquency Prevention, provides quick and easy access to juvenile justice information and resources. Available publications include the journal *Juvenile Justice* and numerous reports, summaries, fact sheets, and bulletins. Much of the JJC's information is available on-line and most of its services are free.

Milton S. Eisenhower Foundation
1660 L St. NW, Suite 200
Washington, DC 20036
(202) 429-0440
fax: (202) 452-0169

Dedicated to reducing crime in inner-city neighborhoods through community programs, this foundation supports funding for programs like Head Start and Job Corps in the belief that better education and job opportunities will reduce juvenile crime and violence.

National Council on Crime and Delinquency (NCCD)
685 Market St., Suite 620
San Francisco, CA 94105
(415) 896-6223
fax: (415) 896-5109

The NCCD supports crime prevention programs aimed at strengthening families, reducing school dropout rates, and increasing employment opportunities for low-income youth. It opposes placing minors in adult jails and executing those who have committed capital offenses before the age of eighteen.

National School Safety Center (NSSC)
4165 Thousand Oaks Blvd., Suite 290
Westlake Village, CA 91362
(805) 373-9977
fax: (805) 373-9277

The NSSC is a research organization that studies school crime and violence, including hate crimes. The center believes that teacher training is an effective means of reducing these problems. Its publications include the book *Gangs in Schools: Breaking Up Is Hard to Do* and the *School Safety Update* newsletter, which is published nine times a year.

Office of Juvenile Justice and Delinquency Prevention
PO Box 6000
Rockville, MD 20849-6000
(800) 851-3420
fax: (301) 251-5212
e-mail: askncjrs@ncjrs.org
Internet: http://www.ncjrs.org/ojjhome.htm

This is the primary federal agency charged with monitoring and improving the juvenile justice system, and developing and funding programs to prevent and control illegal drug use and serious juvenile crime, including youth gangs. It is a division of the Department of Justice.

Youth Crime Watch of America
9300 S. Dadeland Blvd., Suite 100
Miami, FL 33156
(305) 670-2409
fax: (305) 670-3805

Youth Crime Watch of America strives to give youths the tools and guidance necessary to actively reduce crime and drug use in their schools and communities. Its publications include *Talking to Youth About Crime Prevention*, the workbook *Community Based Youth Crime Watch Program Handbook*, and the motivational video *A Call for Young Heroes*.

Websites

Teen Court
Internet: http://www.ncn.com/~snews/teen/

This website contains a listing of names and addresses of teen courts in the United States that can be contacted for more information on local teen court programs. The site also provides information on starting a teen court.

Suggestions for Further Reading

Scott Barbour and Karin L. Swisher, eds., *Violence*. San Diego: Greenhaven Press, 1996.

Michael D. Biskup and Charles P. Cozic, eds., *Youth Violence*. San Diego: Greenhaven Press, 1992.

Tony Bouza, *A Carpet of Blue: An Ex-Cop Takes a Tough Look at America's Drug Problem*. Minneapolis: Deaconess Press, 1992.

Charles P. Cozic, ed., *Gangs*. San Diego: Greenhaven Press, 1996.

A. E. Sadler, ed., *Juvenile Crime*. San Diego: Greenhaven Press, 1997.

Margot Webb, *Coping with Street Gangs*. New York: Rosen Publishing, 1990.

Works Consulted

Books

Thomas J. Bernard, *The Cycle of Juvenile Justice*. New York: Oxford University Press, 1992.

Léon Bing, *Do or Die*. New York: HarperCollins, 1991.

Chris W. Eskridge, ed., *Criminal Justice Concepts and Issues: An Anthology*. Los Angeles: Roxbury Publishing, 1996.

Margaret O. Hyde, *Kids In and Out of Trouble*. New York: Cobblehill Books, 1995.

Kids and Guns: A National Disgrace, 3rd ed. Washington, DC: Educational Fund to End Handgun Violence, 1993.

Malcolm W. Klein, Cheryl L. Maxson, and Jody Miller, *The Modern Gang Reader*. Los Angeles: Roxbury Publishing, 1995.

Dan Korem, *Suburban Gangs: The Affluent Rebels*. Richardson, TX: International Focus Press, 1994.

Rita Kramer, *At a Tender Age: Violent Youth and Juvenile Justice*. New York: Henry Holt, 1988.

Barry Krisberg and James F. Austin, *Reinventing Juvenile Justice*. Newbury Park, CA: Sage Publications, 1993.

Deborah Prothrow-Stith, *Deadly Consequences: How Violence Is Destroying Our Teenage Population and a Plan to Begin Solving the Problem*. New York: HarperCollins, 1991.

William B. Sanders, *Gangbangs and Drive-Bys: Grounded Culture and Juvenile Gang Violence*. New York: Walter de Gruyter, 1994.

U.S. Bureau of the Census, *Statistical Abstract of the United States: 1995*. Austin, TX: The Reference Press, Inc., 1996.

U.S. Bureau of the Census, *Statistical Abstract of the United States: 1996*. Austin, TX: The Reference Press, Inc., 1996.

Articles

Fox Butterfield, "Computer to Trace Guns That Juveniles Buy," *Saint Paul Pioneer Press*, July 8, 1996.

Diane L. Carroad, "Interviews with Head Start Parents," *Children Today*, May/June 1993.

Ruth Conniff, "Meet the Teens in Lockup," *Progressive*, February 1996.

Elizabeth Dunham, "Bad Girls," *Teen*, August 1995.

Leonard D. Eron, "Parent-Child Interaction, Television Violence, and Aggression of Children," *American Psychologist*, February 1982.

Michael A. Fletcher, "Teen's Maximum Time Draws International Ire, but Little in Community He Shared with Victim," *Washington Post*, June 18, 1997.

James Alan Fox and Glenn Pierce, "The Young Desperados: American Killers Are Getting Younger," *USA Today*, January 1994.

Dorian Friedman, "A Reputation That Outruns Reality," *U.S. News & World Report*, January 25, 1993.

J. S. Fuerst and Roy Petty, "The Best Use of Federal Funds for Early Childhood Education (Head Start)," *Phi Delta Kappan*, June 1996.

Ted Gest, "Crime Time Bomb," *U.S. News & World Report*, March 25, 1996.

Sarah Glazer, "Juvenile Justice," *CQ Researcher*, February 24, 1995.

John Hood, "Caveat Emptor: The Head Start Scam," *USA Today*, May 1993.

Jon D. Hull, "A Boy and His Gun," *Time*, August 2, 1993.

Jeffrey L. Katz, "Bill to Improve Head Start Awaits Clinton Signature," *Congressional Quarterly Weekly Report*, May 14, 1994.

Richard Lacayo, "When Kids Go Bad," *Time*, September 19, 1994.

Mike Males and Fay Docuyanan, "Giving Up on the Young," *Progressive*, February 1996.

Janice Min, "Port in a Storm: At Safe Harbor, Doug and Robbie Smith Help Troubled Boys Stay Afloat," *People Weekly*, December 18, 1995.

Tom Morganthau, "The Lull Before the Storm?" *Newsweek*, December 4, 1993.

Elayne Rapping, "The Family Behind Bars," *Progressive*, September 1996.

Joseph F. Sheley and Victoria E. Brewer, "Possession and Carrying of Firearms Among Suburban Youth," *Public Health Reports*, January/February 1995.

Deborah L. Shelton, "L.A. County Tops Statistics for Gang-Related Crime," *American Medical News*, October 16, 1995.

Chi Chi Sileo, "Violent Offenders Get High on Crime," *Insight*, May 2, 1994.

Bob von Sternberg, "Deadly Business: Drugs, Gangs and Cash Made 1995 Minneapolis' Most Homicidal Year," *Star-Tribune*, December 17, 1995.

"Teen Courts: Do They Work?" *Current Events*, October 10, 1994.

"Teen Juries: Are They Fair?" *Current Events*, November 18, 1996.

Michele Weiner-Dairs, "The Lost Boys," *Ladies' Home Journal*, January 1995.

Reports and Fact Sheets

James C. Howell, "Gangs," *Department of Justice, Office of Juvenile Justice and Delinquency Prevention Fact Sheet #12*, April 1994.

Joseph Moone, "Children in Custody 1991: Private Facilities," *Department of Justice, Office of Juvenile Justice and Delinquency Prevention Fact Sheet #2*, April 1993.

Joseph Moone, "Children in Custody 1991: Public Juvenile Facilities," *Department of Justice, Office of Juvenile Justice and Delinquency Prevention Fact Sheet #5*, September 1993.

Eileen Poe-Yamagata and Jeffrey A. Butts, "Female Offenders in the Juvenile Justice System: Statistic Summary," *Department of Justice, Office of Juvenile Justice and Delinquency Prevention (Series)*, June 1996.

Ramsey County (Minnesota) Community Corrections, *Juvenile Services Report*, 1996.

John J. Wilson, "Serious, Violent, and Chronic Juvenile Offenders: A Comprehensive Strategy," *Department of Justice, Office of Juvenile Justice and Delinquency Prevention Fact Sheet #4*, August 1993.

Index

About the Author

Roger Barr is a writer who lives in St. Paul, Minnesota. He writes on historical, political, business, and social topics. His novel *The Treasure Hunt* was published by Medallion Press in 1992. He has written six other books for Lucent Books: *The Vietnam War, The Importance of Richard Nixon, The Importance of Malcolm X, Radios: Wireless Sound, Cities,* and *The American Frontier.*

Picture Credits

Cover photo: Nina Berman/Sipa Press
©1995 Brent Anderson/Impact Visuals, 91
AP/Wide World Photos, Inc., 14, 36, 43, 46, 55, 64, 66, 81, 83
©1995 Steve Cagan/Impact Visuals, 51, 72
©Donna DeCesare/Impact Visuals, 23
Amy C. Elliott, 29, 86
©1992 Harvey Finkle/Impact Visuals, 28
©1995 Hazel Hankin/Impact Visuals, 78
©1993 F. M. Kearney/Impact Visuals, 59
Library of Congress, 7, 9
©1993 Andrew Lichtenstein/Impact Visuals, 67
©1994 Alain McLaughlin/Impact Visuals, 24
©1996 Alain McLaughlin/Impact Visuals, 56, 68
Ernest Paniccioli/Corbis-Bettmann, 34
©Rick Reinhard/Impact Visuals 1993, 93, 94
©1996 Richard R. Renaldi/Impact Visuals, 33
©1990 Ted Soqui/Impact Visuals, 96
©Helen M. Stummer/Impact Visuals, 39
©1993 Jim Tynan/Impact Visuals, 20
©Jim West/Impact Visuals, 89